Gardening
in the Desert

To Jane + Melanie
With best
wishes
Mary Irish

THE LIVING DESERT
**PALO VERDE
GARDEN CENTER**

47900 Portola Ave.
Palm Desert, Ca

(760) 346-5694

Gardening in the Desert

A Guide to Plant Selection & Care

Mary F. Irish

THE UNIVERSITY OF ARIZONA PRESS

TUCSON

The University of Arizona Press
© 2000 The Arizona Board of Regents
All Rights Reserved

♾ This book is printed on acid-free, archival-quality paper.
Manufactured in the United States of America
06 05 04 03 02 7 6 5 4 3 2

    Library of Congress Cataloging-in-Publication Data
Irish, Mary, 1949–
    Gardening in the desert : a guide to plant selection and care / Mary F. Irish
        p. cm.
Includes index.
    ISBN 0-8165-2057-7 (paper : acid-free paper)
    1. Desert plants—Southwest, New. 2. Native plants for
cultivation—Southwest, New. 3. Desert gardening—Southwest,
New. 4. Native plant gardening—Southwest, New. I. Title
    SB427.5 .I75 2000
    635.9'525'0979—dc21
                        00-008918

British Cataloguing-in-Publication Data
A catalogue record for this book is available from the British Library.

To Gary

Contents

Illustrations

Preface

The idea for this book originated in classes and public-speaking engagements during the time I worked for the Desert Botanical Garden. Audiences constantly requested a book about the experience of gardening in the desert, and I was constantly at a loss. There was no such book, and it became clear that one might be useful. I remember my own entry into desert gardening—how much there was to learn and how few resources there were to help me launch a desert garden.

I was born not to the desert but to central Texas, where it is hot, alternately wet and dry, one of the most difficult gardening climates that I know of. After a stint on the Gulf Coast, I found myself in the low Sonoran Desert, possessing a deep passion for gardening and intrigued by a new place. My husband and I thought our Texas origins would help, and perhaps they did, but not enough. Practice, trial and error, talking to friends and colleagues, and looking at other gardens were the only way to learn.

I believe ardently that we all must garden where we live. Gardens are neither absolutely natural nor wholly man created. They are, instead, like spectacular cooking, in which individual, characteristic flavors are melded and re-formed to create new distinctive tastes. A garden's flavor is concocted of climate, soil, selection of plants, personality and taste of the gardener, and look and feel of the natural landscape where the garden occurs.

Most of us want to have a lovely yard composed of good color and good plants, with birds and other wildlife that add interest to the area, and we want to have all this without exorbitant expenditures of work or water or worry. This book is designed for gardeners who are new to the desert and cannot figure out what to do, as well as for gardeners who have been here a long time but just discovered desert plants. It covers the region known as the low desert, which encompasses the deserts of southern California, most of southern Arizona, especially the Phoenix and Tucson metropolitan areas, and southern New Mexico to El Paso, Texas.

This book is a record of my experience and my opinions. I cannot imagine that everything I say will work for everyone, but I hope that it helps.

Acknowledgments

Just as gardens are made up of countless plants, encounters, and observations, a book is a reflection of all the people, events, and activities that have happened to the author. It is sad but entirely too true that it is impossible to list all the wonderful help that it took to finish a book, and this one is no exception. But a few people stand out.

This book was written while I was on a sabbatical leave from the Desert Botanical Garden, and it would have never been done otherwise. Thanks for the opportunity.

Great gardeners are found in unlikely places, but working around a botanical garden for a long time puts you in contact with dozens of them. To all the volunteers and staff of the Garden, I owe an immense debt of gratitude for always being interested in talking about plants, for sharing stories about their gardens, for being willing to go over their failures and successes. Thanks for all the good times.

This book would never have happened if Ted Anderson had not encouraged me to call a publisher and see about getting it done. You may not remember, but I do. Thanks for the boost.

Carol Schatt read and edited the entire manuscript, and no one could ever give a greater gift of friendship. She made it the book that it is, although I still get to claim all the opinions and all the errors. Sherry New also read the entire manuscript and helped by listening through the tough times. Thanks for everything.

And, of course, thanks to Bob for showing me that challenges make for confidence and with confidence comes good work.

But no one has had a greater role in all aspects of this book or my gardening life than my beloved gardening partner, Gary. He is the best plantsman I know, even though I veto more than half his ideas for the garden. Thanks is too pale a word for his encouragement, endless assistance, and steady support during the development of this book and our garden.

Gardening in the Desert

Purple prickly pear (Opuntia violaceae) *and* Agave weberi MARY IRISH

1 *Conditions of Desert Gardening*

$\mathcal{M}$y mother is still trying to figure out what I see in this place. As we drive around the area, she cannot resist exulting, "Oh, good, there is something green!" or "Oh, doesn't that green look good!" whenever possible. She is not alone in this feeling. Countless new residents arrive in the low desert, thinking of thrusting their hands into the dirt to create a new garden in their new home, and are chagrined to learn that nothing seems to grow for them here. Failure piles up on failure; old favorites burn up in the heat; trees and shrubs fail to thrive; annuals planted during benevolent March turn to dust by May; dirt more nearly resembles construction material; and the sky never seems to cloud over and rain.

Amid such frustrating foreignness, new gardeners become increasingly disheartened. Many return to familiar habits and apply copious amounts of water to grow the gardens they desire. But nostalgic lawns and garden magazine annuals do not fit the look of a desert city and require shocking amounts of water. Other immigrants to the desert eschew intense watering in favor of sere, flat, gravel-covered yards with a solitary cactus, a lonely mesquite, and a few small boulders. This type of yard is certainly water efficient, but it fails to reflect the rich possibilities of desert flora and is neither inviting nor comfortable.

Where are the flavor and form of the Moorish gardens that achieved exquisite success in similar climates hundreds of years ago? Where are the echoes of the great Spanish-Mexican cultural blend so evident in food and architecture but so weakly acknowledged in our gardens? In a climate so hospitable to outdoor living, why are gardens so severe and unfriendly? Is it that difficult to garden in the desert or to grow desert plants?

No, it is not. I think the key to more satisfying and rewarding gardening in a desert environment lies in selecting garden plants from the vast array of species native to the deserts and semiarid regions of the world rather than relying on plants from milder, wetter, and more temperate climes. Desert and semiarid species have proved their ability to thrive in rigorous conditions. The gardener sacrifices nothing in function, form, or beauty by using these plants; in fact, they are some of the most luscious bloomers and have the most graceful forms and outstanding performance available to gardeners anywhere. In addition, the diversity of desert plants is rapidly increasing as more plants from arid regions of the world are becoming available.

The increasing use of desert plants in the American Southwest is building a new tradition in desert gardening and a strong regional style. The use of diverse succulents gives the arid garden a character, form, and substance quite different from that of the frothy, leaf-dominated gardens of the eastern United States. The sharp, hard edges of yuccas and agaves, with their intense symmetry, strong colors, and unexpected or vivid color combinations, lend a wide range of styles and forms to the desert garden.

In the low desert, gardening is a year-round activity, not so seasonally driven as temperate zone gardening. Spring regales the area with a magnificent, although short, bloom season, followed by the sensational late-spring bloom of cacti. Then a glorious fall bloom, especially among Chihuahuan shrubs, is followed by the long winter bloom of various South African species. And regardless of how desperately hot and dry, summer is a feast of blooming plants.

Rocks should play a large role in the desert garden because they form the very architecture of our region. Distant, gargantuan mountains of rock outline the horizon; closer, they define a stream or the side of a hill. The intermittent placement of rocks in a garden provides dozens of tiny microclimates, which in turn make for greater species diversity. I had a fine friend who grew the most perfect agaves. He maintained that his success came from surrounding the base of the plants with rocks, which cooled the roots below. Looking at his results, I believed him.

Gardening in the arid West is far different from gardening in all other regions of this country. Generally, the advice and information given in national magazines, seed catalogs, and books are ineffective in this region. Following those guidelines often leads to failure, frustration, and the conclusion that there can be no satisfactory gardening in the desert. Nothing could be further from the truth. Just as eastern American gardeners once struggled to release the firm bonds of English gardening traditions that did not work here, so, too, must western, and especially desert, gardeners free themselves from the expectations and routines determined by the conditions of the eastern United States and discover the delights and joys of the gardens that are possible in the arid West.

So I urge everyone who begins gardening here to start with an understanding of the conditions incumbent in the low desert regions of the American Southwest. They are:

- ❀ a long growing season highlighted by a long, hot summer
- ❀ soils that are low in organic content and highly alkaline
- ❀ meager annual rainfall with long periods of time between rains

Desert garden scene **GARY IRISH**

These conditions dictate new ground rules for gardening:

- ❦ The seasons are different here than elsewhere.
- ❦ Shade is highly desirable.
- ❦ Plants of desert origin already have the necessary adaptations to live successfully in these conditions.
- ❦ Supplemental irrigation, at least to some extent, is a way of life.

Weather...

I vividly remember the first time I stepped into the Arizona sunshine. I had been considering a move here, and this was the trip to see if I liked it. It was Memorial Day, and when I walked off the plane and onto the tarmac at Sky Harbor Airport in Phoenix, the sheer brilliance of the light overwhelmed me. Colors were deep and intense, the air was sharp, edges were crisp and detailed, and it was quite hot. I did not know until later that this experience encapsulated the nature and style of heat in the desert.

Most people are astonished by the extreme high temperatures that occur in the desert, mistakenly believing that triple-digit temperatures are unbearable. The cry of "It's a dry heat!" echoes far and wide, and there is truth in it. Low relative humidity does make higher temperatures more comfortable than might seem possible, but for gardeners such low humidity is one of the most difficult conditions for growing plants.

Plants continually lose water vapor from the stomata of their leaves as a by-product of photosynthesis. When it is warm and sunny, plants photosynthesize at a great rate and lose a good deal of water vapor. When the relative humidity is low—meaning, there is little water vapor in the air—the rate of loss is accelerated and water loss occurs at a rate far faster than can be replaced in the plant.

Plants that are from desert regions combat this circumstance with a host of adaptations. Many succulents have rearranged their photosynthetic schedule so their stomata open at night, when cooler temperatures lower the rate of evaporation. Countless desert plants have small umbrellas of hairs on their leaves that cool and shade these tiny faucets. These hairs are the source of the gray leaf color so common in desert plants. Other plants, like jojoba, can turn their leaves away from the glare of the sun. Many plants have developed a waxy cuticle on the leaf to slow the rate of release of water vapor, which is why so many desert plants have sturdy, hard leaves. Others, such as the ocotillo, shed their leaves until a more favorable time. Palo verde trees concentrate the cells that perform photosynthesis in their bark. In this way the tree can continue to grow and sustain itself without leaves, which have a higher rate of evaporation.

Plants that are not from desert regions do not enjoy these physical adaptations and consequently have a difficult time with desert conditions, especially in the summer. As their need for water increases, they wilt, a condition that a plant can tolerate only a few times before it loses vigor. Sunburn and heat stress add to the problem, so that by the end of June these plants are crispy memories in the garden.

There are two summer seasons in the low desert—the hot, dry early summer, which begins in May, and the summer thunderstorm season, which begins as early as July. Early summer is a particularly rigorous time for plants, even desert species. Long days with highs above 107°F and relative humidity of 12 percent or lower simply wear plants out. Leaves fade and yellow like the pages of an old album. Plants that go dormant in the summer become ghosts around the garden, stark forms set on a schedule of endurance against what I call the "Big Heat." During this first summer season, just one day's loss of irrigation can be devastating to new plants or those in containers. Few plants can survive transplanting during this time unless drastic measures are taken for their survival. Watering well is extremely important; a light mist in the early morning or a late evening spray is often helpful just to cool things down. Plants grow little during this time; the objective is to keep them healthy and alive.

Around July the second summer begins. With a rise in humidity, clouds begin to form and the summer thunderstorm season, known locally as the monsoon, is underway. At this time a different kind of heat stirs in the garden. Beginning in the southern part of the state in early July and moving northward through August and early September, the rains are a fickle phenomenon, skirting one area and deluging another on the same day. The rain may be erratic, but the increase in humidity is certain.

The humid air provides a marked relief to plants, and most gardeners notice a decided uplift in their gardens. Warm-season growers and cold-tender plants can be transplanted at this time. When the rains are good, many desert shrubs, particularly those from the Chihuahuan Desert, such as Texas rangers and daleas, come into bloom.

Perversely, this is also the season gardeners must watch for root infections and rot. Most desert plants, especially large woody ones, need less water during this season than during the early summer, so adjusting a watering or irrigation schedule is important at this time.

The single best mitigator of the heat is shade, whether provided by porches, shade cloth, or another plant. Shade helps everything. Cacti, agaves, aloes, and other succulents, as well as perennials and even larger shrubs grow well in light shade. The relief shade provides is more than just a gentle cooling; it is a soothing balm, felt in your eyes, on your head, and around your skin, offering a break from the unremitting, determined pulse of the sun.

The shade from trees or any other plant works in two ways. Trees emit minuscule amounts of water vapor from each leaf stoma during transpiration, creating barely noticeable but effective evaporative cooling. In addition, tree leaves absorb the sun's radiation, harvesting that energy for photosynthesis and reducing the surface temperature of a plant leaf or a human arm under the shield of the tree.

These small benevolences of shade can make the difference between healthy, vigorous plants and those that are continually stressed and ragged. The light shade of leguminous trees, such as mesquite and palo verde, breaks up the sun's bright light and cools the ground, yet permits enough light to penetrate the canopy to encourage good growth among any plants growing below.

After the intensity of summer, the low desert and its gardeners are ready to enjoy a long, mild, cool season, one of the best winter climates in the world. Fall and winter are sunny most of the time, and temperatures are mild, creating ideal conditions for growth in a wide range of desert plants. Rain in this season is unreliable, in some years bountiful, in others scarce. Winter rains are gentle and can last all day, soaking deep into the soil and replenishing the soil moisture necessary to the survival of large shrubs and trees.

Soils...

Soils in desert regions are low in organic content, are alkaline, often develop a hard crust on the surface, and frequently are underlaid by an impermeable layer called "caliche." Sometimes they are quite shallow. That may sound daunting, but with a few basic techniques, the gardener can make the most of desert soils.

There are two reasons for the low organic content of desert soils. First, there are relatively fewer plants to decompose and provide the basic organic content, and second, high temperatures rapidly break down what little organic matter there is. In addition, lack of moisture slows decomposition. Just how slowly is vividly demonstrated by Christmas trees left in the alley in January that are perfect brown fossils in July, or fallen citrus fruits neglected under the tree that become brown and rock hard.

For the gardener this means that adding organic matter is a constant part of soil maintenance. You cannot add too much organic matter to the soil, particularly in the form of compost. In areas where soils are a compacted clay, compost or other organic matter opens up the structure of the soil, allowing more water and air into the tiny interspaces of the soil, improving drainage and nutrient absorption. In rocky or sandy soils, compost and organic matter add nutrients and slow the runoff of water, so that a plant's roots can take up necessary minerals and water.

Mulching is also a highly desirable practice in low desert regions. Mulch made up of organic matter eventually breaks down, releasing nutrients and creating better soil. Even inorganic mulches, popular in Arizona as decomposed granite (which I admit sounds like an oxymoron) or rocks, perform the principal function of mulch, which is to shade and therefore cool the surface of the soil, significantly slowing the rate of water evaporation.

When I was a girl, it was common to train left-handed children to write with their right hand, and I had a girlfriend who endured this ridiculous ordeal. She dutifully wrote her lessons with her right hand, but outside school she pitched softball, ate dinner, and fastened her clothing with her left hand. Back then I thought it was enviable to be able to use each hand so ably; now I think it is lunacy to try to run so far away from what is inherent. And so it is with soils out here in the desert.

Soils in the desert are alkaline, which means that they fall above 7 on the pH scale. Soils with a pH reading of 7.5 and below are acidic. Like dominant hands, a soil is acidic or alkaline according to its origins and chemistry, and while it can be adjusted in limited areas, such as a raised bed, containers, or a tiny corner, the fix is fleeting: alkalinity is permanent. The addition of acidifying products works for a short time, but they must be replenished continually.

Plants are either equipped by their inherent biochemistry to grow and thrive in alkaline soils or they are not. The character of the soil is the single best reason to use desert species in your garden. Such plants are well adapted and capable of looking stunning in desert soils.

Gardeners throughout desert regions have struggled with a plant condition known as chlorosis. Chlorosis is a symptom of a mineral deficiency in plants, and in the low desert the most common form is iron deficiency. Symptoms include young leaves that are yellow with veins that remain green. In extreme cases the entire leaf becomes yellow-white, so pale as to be translucent.

The problem is not that the soil is deficient in iron—there is plenty of iron in desert soils. Rather, it is the type of iron compounds that are present in alkaline soils. Plants that become chlorotic are unable to take up iron as it naturally occurs. Adding chelated iron certainly can help and often appears to fix the problem, but the fix is temporary. Without constant replenishment and occasionally even with it, the plant struggles, languishes, and dies.

Nothing can permanently alter the chemistry of a plant, and it is usually impractical to alter the chemistry of the soil in your garden. So, like left-handed children struggling to be right-handed, poorly adapted plants will look fine only as long as iron is being added, but the fact that the plants are so poorly adapted will eventually come home. They will fail to thrive because they are living in continuous low-level stress. Their life span will be shortened, and frequently their ultimate height. A clear example of this phenomenon is the queen palm *(Syagrus romanzoffiana)* in the Phoenix area, which is often pitiful, stunted, and yellowing, living a scant 20 years. Nevertheless, queen palms are popularly sold and planted.

Soils in the low desert are remarkably variable in their physical structure, ranging from a tight, dense clay to a loose, rocky soil that is often very shallow. In the basin and range topography so common in the arid West, clay soils occur mainly in the lower basins, between buttes and small mountains. These soils hold moisture extremely well—too well. They also can stay cold longer than other soils. When dried-out clay soils form a hard crust at the surface, water may be unable to penetrate, preventing deep percolation. Clay soils are greatly improved by the addition of organic matter, such as mulch, compost, manure, and leaves.

There are sandy loam or clay loam soils in the region, but these treasures are uncommon except near old watercourses. More common are sandy to rocky soils with or without caliche. These are fairly young soils that result from the washing down of mountains and ridges into smaller and smaller parts. Water moves through them very well—in extreme cases, too well. These soils have little organic content; generous doses of organic material applied at least annually can help to improve them by increasing their moisture-holding capacity and nutrients. To the surprise of many novice desert gardeners, plants grow well in sandy to rocky soils. In fact, desert species thrive in these soils, with their combination of open drainage and lighter texture.

In many areas, especially on slopes and ridges, you may encounter the bane of desert gardening, a lens or layer of calcium carbonate known as caliche. Sometimes caliche is thin, nothing more than a layer at or near the surface, and can be broken up and moved aside. My garden is riddled with caliche of this type, which is the easiest to manage; hard digging moves it out of the way. In one area of the yard, however, it took three weeks to complete digging a hole, using a 27-pound iron bar to fracture and bust up the caliche. This terrifying tool, called a caliche bar, is an absolute requirement for any gardener living in an area of extensive caliche.

Caliche also can be a deep layer 3 or more feet thick, an impenetrable barrier that no amount of digging can remove. There is a good adage to remember when dealing with caliche soils: If water cannot penetrate, neither can roots. Fill a hole and let it drain a few hours or overnight. If all the water does not drain, there is nothing to do but relocate the plant.

Water...

To say that this region has low rainfall is like observing that it is cold in Antarctica. Phoenix expects an annual rainfall of about 7.5 inches. When I lived in New Orleans, we expected that much rain in an average storm. In addition, the rain is not spread evenly throughout the year. About two-thirds falls in the winter and about one-third during the summer monsoon. This leaves anywhere from three to five months at a time with no rainfall at all. Tucson and other places at slightly higher elevations receive more rain overall, up to 12 inches per year, with more falling during the summer monsoon than in winter. The El Paso region also receives more rain in the summer and has occasional winter storms, and areas to the west, such as Palm Springs, receive all of their 3 to 4 inches per year in the winter.

This means that some supplemental irrigation is necessary to maintain a healthy garden. It is therefore important that gardeners in desert regions attempt to use and save as much rainwater as possible and irrigate most efficiently.

Retaining and using rainwater can be done in various ways: by using basins or berms around individual plants to capture rainwater during its infrequent appearances, by contouring on steep slopes, and by building check dams to slow water down and allow for deep percolation. Reservoirs, ponds, and rain barrels can be used to collect and hold rainwater for future use in the garden.

The most efficient way to irrigate plants is to deliver water directly to the root system, minimizing surface evaporation. This can be done with a drip irrigation system but can be accomplished just as well by placing a hose directly on the ground and running it slowly for a long time. A long time for a tree, large shrub, or mature succulent is at least three hours or overnight; for a smaller perennial it is up to one hour.

Drip irrigation was developed in Israel for agriculture but has become popular anywhere water is scarce. The vocabulary of drip irrigation is like a secret code among long-time desert gardeners. *How much gpm? What is the volume? Is it variable? My flags are reversed, Hand me the punch,* and *Where is the spaghetti?* are a smattering of the colorful phrases from this irrigation technique.

Drip irrigation essentially delivers water directly to the root zone of a plant via a system of flexible tubing with ever-decreasing diameters, much of it buried underground. At the delivery point to each plant, the water drips through a minute hole or emitter at a prescribed rate, usually 1 or 2 gallons per hour. Unlike with sprayers and sprinklers, all water coming out of the system goes to the plant's root zone. On a summer day more than 60 percent of the water from a sprinkler is lost to evaporation, whereas surface evaporation with a drip system is negligible.

Drip systems deliver water so slowly that it penetrates into the ground, moving down the soil column into the root zone, where a plant truly needs the water. Fast-running hoses and sprinklers mimic a hard rain; great quantities of water fall on hard ground and run off or evaporate before plants can use it.

Drip irrigation systems can be managed with battery or electrically driven timers, which offer convenience and reliability, as well as assurance that plants are receiving only the amount of water desired—no more, no less. After enduring the slavery of hand-watering a yard full of desert perennials, I can heartily recommend a good drip system. It allows you to reclaim your life.

However, the single most effective water conservation strategy is to use plants that do not require excessive amounts of supplemental irrigation to look their best. And most of those plants are denizens of the American deserts: the Mohave, in the western edge of the region, with the driest and coldest weather; the Sonoran, in the middle, which has the most varied and numerous flora; and the Chihuahuan, on the eastern edge, which has contributed many of the most common desert ornamentals.

When I moved to Arizona and began work at the Desert Botanical Garden on its plant sales, about 150 species of desert plants were available to the desert gardener. Ten years later more than 400 species were offered, and more good desert plants are being developed all the time. As these plants appear in retail yards and at large national garden centers, it is testament to the increasing acceptance of and interest in desert plants by the gardening public. Desert plants are used not because they are hallmarks of a noble cause but because they offer great color, variety, and beauty; excellent pest and disease resistance; and low water use. They are helping us create some of the most beautiful regional gardens in this country.

2 Trees

*I*n a perennial bed near the house, the four-year-old camelthorn (*Acacia erioloba*) was sagging yet again, shaggy with new growth, inadequately supported, and buffeted by summer storms. It was clear that within two years the branches would begin to mingle with the power lines and pruning would become nearly impossible. Already the tree was more of a gangly, thorny pole than the crowning garland I had envisioned for this bed. The conclusion was inescapable: I had put a fine tree in a terrible place. I cut it down that very day.

Acacia roots give off a revolting stench when they are cut, and I felt the awful smell was retribution for the pathetic ending I had brought to this beloved tree species. But I learned once again that a beautiful plant grown in the wrong situation becomes a mocking monstrosity of its own grace and appeal. Nowhere does this kind of error haunt a gardener more than in the placement and selection of trees.

Ideally, a tree should fit so well in the landscape that it seems obvious, like the pure finish of a steeple on a church or the perfect gate. Badly placed trees are absurd giants looming over a tiny house like a huge animal cramped in a small pen, waiting to burst out, or they are pitiful, isolated specimens too delicate to do more than fade into irrelevance, petulant and spoiled.

It is therefore important to consider not only a tree's ultimate size but its shape, leaf style, and color—as well as what will be over, under, and around it—before giving it dominion over your garden. And a tree should conform not only in size but in attitude. Big trees demand big space; light, delicate trees work best in intimate surroundings; thorny trees are ruthless next to walkways and play areas; a tree in the middle of a view does not frame or enhance it; and gardens dominated by native desert plantings look ludicrous with tall, large-leaved, tropical trees.

Trees provide one of the most effective ways to screen out ugly views or tall intrusions, such as power lines. This is particularly true of desert trees, with their strong propensity to grow multiple branches and low limbs. But trees can just as effectively screen out desirable mountain views and starry skies if put in their way. There is a main thoroughfare in Phoenix that has a dramatic curve with a joyous view of the bold thrust of the McDowell Mountains. This

Velvet mesquite (Prosopis velutina) **MARY IRISH**

view captures the unique beauty of the city, highlighting the rise of the arid mountains and their fall to broad plains. A row of newly planted trees is destined to obliterate the view when they reach maturity, breaking the connection between the majesty of the area mountains and the landscapes of the low desert.

Wildlife, especially birds and the insects on which they thrive, fill the garden that has a healthy complement of trees. Trees offer shelter, roosts, nest sites, and food. Coveys of neighborhood quail use our mesquites as their sentinel tower; mockingbirds, thrashers, and towhees race through the palo verdes and acacias throughout the day. It was a happy day indeed when one of our mesquites grew large enough to entice doves to roost in it.

In our desert, trees take on nearly mystical significance in the garden as providers of shade that tames the relentless desert heat and moderates the blinding desert light. Shade in a desert garden spells the difference between a comfortable, enjoyable, usable place and one that is blistering empty ground. Shade is not a problem but a solution. The shade from a tree's canopy cools the ground underneath, allowing it to hold a fraction more moisture; minute amounts of water vapor exuding from thousands of leaves cool the air ever so slightly. The ground under trees collects a cascade of spent blooms, ripe seeds, and withered leaves; if allowed to slowly rot, such droppings make the soil hospitable to a great diversity of plants. Plants grown in light shade lose less moisture and are less likely to sunburn. Everything in desert gardens responds to a fine drift of shade.

In winter, evergreen trees and the dense branches of most desert trees provide enough frost protection for subtropical plants growing below them. Freezes in the desert are the result of radiant cooling, in which warmed air from the earth rises quickly through the clear, cold night sky. A tree blocks this movement and shoves the slightly warmer air back down around the plants.

The microclimate created by this overhead protection can be highly dramatic. I recall the winter that I arranged a selection of potted aloes, extras from the Desert Botanical Garden's collection, under a wide mesquite. There were hard freezes that winter that decimated the mother plants in the open ground while the potted offspring remained unharmed beneath the mesquite boughs.

Planting...

The relocation of large trees, often sold in boxes from 24 to more than 60 inches wide, has become something of a trend in the desert areas of Arizona, Nevada, and southern California. This "bigger is better—I want something I can enjoy and see now" planting craze is so unabashedly accepted that arguing against it seems as tasteless as ribald humor at a funeral. But how can we regard a tree that has grown in a particular spot for over a hundred years, developing over that time a distinctive gnarled trunk, spectacular girth, and graceful form, as being "saved" when it is uprooted and mutilated in order to be put into a garden? I have nagging doubts about the long-term health and life span of these uprooted giants. Moreover, I think such an approach is the antithesis of real gardening, in which you develop and nurture a set of plants through long association; the chorus of associated plants in the garden, living and dead, melds into a wonderful, compatible song about the land, telling not only of its present but of its history.

We seem to have lost the gift of patience, of waiting for time to unfold its story. Instant gardens planted with impatience and with scant attention to gentle development are disconnected and sterile; the personality and interest of the gardener are absent. Beverly Nichols recounts in *Merry Hall,* his "Tale of the Thirty Cypress," that in order to increase the number of trees in his wood, he planted a flat of seeds from a large ancient cypress on the property. He was surprised but pleased to find that his seeds became small plants, his small plants grew, and in the end he had the forest he desired. In later years and later books, he retold this tale again and again, remembering that once he "held the entire forest in the palm of my hand." I cannot imagine such a thing happening today in any new garden, public or private.

It will come as no surprise that I fall squarely into the plant-them-small camp and take as canon that a tree in a 5-gallon container is the ideal size for planting. The smaller a tree is planted, the better its chances of survival and good root establishment, and the more likely that it will grow straight and strong and live a long time. No matter what size, transplanting is a shock for trees as well as humans, and recovery and regrowth are easier the younger you are.

A plant in a 15-gallon pot or one in a 24-inch box may look larger, but check carefully to be sure the roots are likewise larger; the size of the top is largely irrelevant when you are purchasing a tree. Plants that are leaping out of pots or that look too big for the pot may be overgrown. Examine the bottom of the pot and take the tree out of it if you can. You should see that the roots are growing to the edge of the soil and filling the pot without crowding or circling. If the roots are crawling through the bottom or circling around the pot, pick another specimen. It is difficult, often impossible, to retrain girdled roots to relax and grow straight again.

Planting a tree in your garden is not difficult or tricky. The only real hazard is caliche, that ghastly impenetrable layer of calcium carbonate that occurs regularly but at erratic depths throughout the region. There is no way to get rid of caliche; you have to work with it.

To evaluate whether a tree will be able to grow satisfactorily where caliche is present, dig the planting hole, fill it with water, and watch how long it takes to drain. The longer it takes, the poorer the drainage; a hole that has no significant change in water level after standing overnight is hopeless for a tree. Plant the tree elsewhere and choose something with a smaller root system for your original hole.

Sometimes a hole, or chimney, can be punched through a small segment of caliche to allow both water and eventually roots to penetrate. But the sad fact is that if water cannot find a way out, neither can roots.

Recent research from around the country has demonstrated that a hole roughly four to five times as wide as the diameter of the tree's container and as deep as the soil in the container is the best size for root establishment. A wide but not particularly deep planting hole creates an excellent zone for lateral root growth. Lateral roots are what hold a plant in place, and from them grow the tiny feeder roots that absorb water and nutrients. Amazingly enough, tree roots usually are not terribly deep, often as shallow as 8 inches and rarely deeper than 36 inches, so a wide lateral root system is important.

Besides checking for drainage, there is another good reason to fill a new hole with water and let the water drain completely: the plant will be planted in wet soil. This is a particularly good practice when the weather is warm and the chances for wilting are high. Remove the tree from the pot, place it in the hole, and backfill with moist soil, tamping the dirt down every 6 inches or so to eliminate as many air pockets as you can. The soil will not subside so far into the hole as it dries and will help keep the tree upright. Take care to plant the tree at the same level in the ground as it was in the pot.

You can add compost or forest mulch to the backfill, up to 25 percent by volume, but it is not absolutely necessary. Using more than that, especially in unamended native soils, discourages roots to reach beyond the highly enriched soil, and they can settle into a kind of isolation, failing to grow beyond the original hole. Likewise, if the backfill in the hole holds more water than the surrounding soil, roots will not grow outward into the surrounding arid soil. A large tree with a tiny root system will fall over in the first strong summer windstorm. I personally have never seen amendments such as vitamins have any real effect.

While backfilling, build a small basin around the tree, roughly the diameter of the drip line and 3 to 4 inches deep. Water thoroughly after you finish planting. If the tree leans or seems top-heavy, prune back the long branches until the tree stands upright on its own.

The best time of year to plant a tree begins in September and continues through the cool season. The danger of frost makes late December and January a bit tricky, but the season continues through March. After March it is essential to pay close attention to watering.

Cool-season planting allows time for a vigorous root system to develop before the rigors of the long desert summer begin. Winters are so mild that some growth is likely even then. Soil moisture lasts twice as long as during the warm season, reducing the possibilities of wilting leaves and drying roots.

Staking...

One of the reasons I so strongly favor planting smaller trees is that they require less staking and grow to have strong trunks in the course of their life. I cringe when I see plants supported by a single stake attached directly to the trunk. These plants cannot move in the wind and will easily snap and break. Tree wood gains strength from being buffeted in the wind, so give your tree every opportunity to toughen up. If staking is necessary, use two stakes placed opposite each other and perpendicular to the prevailing wind, 2 to 3 feet from the trunk. Tie the tree to one stake low on the trunk, using tree tape or other material that will not cut into the bark. Tie the tree to the other stake about 2 feet higher, using the same kind of tying material. Staking need not be left in place for more than three or four months; by that time there should be ample roots to hold the tree up.

Watering...

A tree uses more water than any other plant except lawn grass. Therefore it makes sense to use trees that are adapted to desert conditions for the greatest possible water conservation. Learning to water appropriately, both when and how much, is one of the most daunting challenges for the desert gardener. Too little or too infrequent water and the plants will fail to thrive or, worse, will die; too much water and they will rot or bolt out of the ground, creating havoc in the garden.

If you watch the growth of untended native mesquites, you will notice that they don't grow steadily; they grow in rapid bursts. Their growth spurts are almost always the result of a good, long soaking during warm weather. These trees are sturdy, have heavy trunks and great form, and it is unusual to find one blown over by the wind.

Many ornamental trees, however, are kept continually moist. They are watered too frequently, typically two or three times a week, on systems that deliver light, shallow watering. As a result, they grow much more crown than root. Soon the tree becomes immense, with long extended whips for branches, and resembles a whirligig atop a stick. While it may seem satisfying to see "how fast that tree is growing," it is a near certainty that without commensurate growth in the root system, the tree will topple over during the first really strong wind.

So what will correct this overgrowth and the resulting loss of tree to wind? Oddly enough, I am convinced the answer lies in watering less often and more deeply.

Newly planted trees need to be watered often for a year or two. After the second year in the ground, the time between waterings should be extended, but the duration of the waterings should be long, slow, and deep. This watering method will promote the combination of a well-grown root system with a balanced spreading crown. Desert trees in particular respond much better to a deep soaking at fairly lengthy intervals. Like all good things, trees don't grow well in a hurry, and the more patience you exercise, the better the tree and the longer it will live. Well-grown trees do not require nearly so much pruning, staking, and maintenance and have a greater likelihood of surviving into a majestic old age.

I have reluctantly included a watering table (see p. 20), but it comes with a warning: all watering recommendations are general and cannot account for the vagaries of soil, temperature, size, and watering instruments. I cannot stress enough that you must watch your plants, see how they are doing, and adjust any watering guide to suit you and your garden.

Any watering regime for established trees (those that have been in the landscape about two years), including that described in the table, is hard to achieve with drip irrigation. Drip irrigation delivers a small amount of water at fairly steady intervals and works extremely well for more shallow-rooted plants like perennials and vegetables. If you use a drip system for your trees, be sure that the emitters deliver a large enough volume for trees, 3 to 5 gallons per hour for small trees and up to 10 gallons per hour for larger ones. This can be accomplished by spacing several emitters around the tree, by using emitters that deliver a large volume of water, or by greatly extending the amount of time the line runs. When using several emitters, space them around the tree so that it gets water uniformly on all sides.

TIMETABLE FOR WATERING DESERT TREES
(Assume a new tree in a 15-gallon or smaller container)

Age of Tree	How Often	When
First Year (spring planting)	every day	first week after planting
	twice a week	through June
	once a week	July—September
	twice a month	October—November and March—April
	once a month	December—February
First Year (fall planting)	twice a week	for 1 month
	once a week	for next month
	twice a month	December—March
	3 times a month	April—May
	once a week	June—September
Second Year through 3 to 5 Years of Age	twice a month	April—September
	once a month	October—March
After 3 to 5 Years or When Tree Is 10 to 12 Feet Tall	once a month	May—September
	once every 2 months	October—April
Fully Established Trees	once a month	May—July or as weather dictates

Regardless of what technique you use, a tree should be watered long enough and slowly enough for the water to penetrate 2 to 3 feet and cover the entire root zone. Therefore, if you use an automated drip system, dedicate one station solely to trees. Drip systems with one valve or station serving the entire yard deliver too much water to some of the plants and too little to others, and the results are never satisfactory.

I use a hose to water trees after their first year and leave it on the tree for hours, often overnight, on a very slow trickle. While I prefer hand-watering trees, this method does have its drawbacks, and one of them is my increasing tendency to forget what I am doing. After diligently searching for a water leak throughout the garden, I have found that a slow trickle I left on a tree 36 hours earlier was the cause. Be smarter—use some kind of timer.

The old adage about watering at the drip line is an adequate rule of thumb for a newly planted or young tree. The strategy becomes even more effective when you use basins to trap and hold water so that it can percolate at a leisurely pace instead of running off. But whether a tree is watered by basin, drip irrigation line, or hose, as it grows, so must the area that is watered. The roots nearest the tree are woody, meant to serve as anchors. The roots at the margins do the work of water and nutrient uptake and respiration, and that is where your tree needs the water. So as the tree grows, the basin must be expanded to accommodate its larger size and larger root zone.

Most desert trees can be taken off supplemental watering after they reach about 6 inches in trunk diameter and 10 to 12 feet in height. By then they should be able to live on natural rainfall supplemented by monthly deep soaks during the hottest part of the summer. This summer irrigation maximizes the vigor and health of a tree and goes a long way toward extending its life in the garden.

Pruning...

Because most trees need pruning from time to time, it is wise to understand what pruning can do for your tree. First and foremost, it promotes the health of a tree. Deadwood, crossed branches that can rub and create wounds, and diseased or torn parts should be removed to maintain the tree's vigor and prevent disease. In addition, pruning a tree gently over time permits the tree and the garden to meld together, conforming to the needs of the garden while retaining the distinctive form of the tree.

Sadly, it is not difficult to find appalling examples of ill-considered pruning. I know of a palo verde that looks like a giraffe: two great branches nearly 40 feet tall are entirely naked, with not a branch between them except at the very top. I can show you a mesquite that a pruner, when faced with a choice between a large lateral branch and a tall, upright one, removed half of the upright one, leaving a bizarre tree form. And everywhere you can find examples of trees that grew too tall for the eaves or the power line and were cut straight across, just below the overhang.Pruning is an art, but good pruning can be learned by any of us. There are only a few things to remember:

- ❦ Prune to a junction.
- ❦ Prune to leave the branch collar intact.
- ❦ Do not prune beyond the collar into the joining branch.
- ❦ Use the sharpest tool you have and the right size for the job.
- ❦ Leave a smooth cut and eschew the use of wound treatments.
- ❦ Prune by hand—power tools are for firewood.

Mesquites, palo verdes, ironwoods, acacias, and most other desert species are best pruned in spring or summer. Because they are rarely, if ever, completely dormant and most are briefly deciduous when the weather is cold, pruning in the winter is inadvisable and can encourage infection and other dieback problems. Try to take as little as possible at one time, and don't remove more than about one-fourth of the mass of the tree in a season. If the damage to a tree is from frost, resist the temptation to "pretty it up" until all danger of frost is past.

Tree Choices...

Mesquites

Treasured by countless American cultures before Europeans arrived, mesquites are fittingly known as the "tree of life." Able to grow in harsh conditions and any kind of soil, mesquites have earned their place as the most common desert tree used ornamentally. Mesquites have pointed the way to reliable sources of water for centuries because they occur in washes, drainages, and along the banks of major watercourses.

Native peoples used all parts of the tree: to build shelter, to burn as firewood, to make dyes and medicines, and perhaps most important, to store as food. They gathered the fallen mesquite pods, or beans, and ground them into a flour. Mesquite flour is delicious; at first it tastes slightly bitter and earthy, but within moments the flavor turns smooth and sweet. Mesquite flour makes a delightful addition to muffins, breads, pancakes, and cookies. Ancestral desert people made the flour by pounding the pods on a stone metate, but with a nod to twentieth-century convenience, I find that a blender works just as well. Native American cooks mixed the flour with water to form dense cakes about the size of a hockey puck, which they stored for use throughout the year.

The Spanish took to this tree immediately, corrupting the Nahuatl name, *mizquitl,* into the common name we use today. They built everything with it, indoors and out, and the cattle they brought to the New World fed readily on its pods.

The American Southwest is home to four mesquites, but there are about 40 species found throughout Mexico, Central America, and South America.

Velvet mesquite *(Prosopis velutina)* is the most commonly encountered mesquite throughout the low elevations of the southwestern United States, and for my money it is the best all-round choice as a shade tree. A handsome, often multitrunked tree with intriguingly gnarled stems, the velvet mesquite has leaves composed of a forked pair of pinnae, each of which holds a various

Palo blanco (Acacia willardiana) **GARY IRISH**

count of leaflets in up to 30 pairs. The rich gray-green leaflets have a coating of abundant fine hairs. Collectively, these hairs produce the delicate feeling that is the origin of the common name. This is the species of the old bosques of central and southern Arizona, huge forests of mesquite that once lined all the major watercourses in the lower parts of the state. This species yields the sweetest pods for mesquite flour, and from it bees make wonderful honey.

As a garden tree, the velvet mesquite is graceful, with flowing dark-barked stems spreading into a fine shady canopy from an extensive crown. Mature trees are generally 25 to 30 feet tall, but plants growing near permanent water have been recorded at up to 50 feet tall. Multiple stems are common; regular and early pruning will help shape and direct the tree to suit your garden. Trees with double stems that fork low to the ground often split at this weak spot, so it is advisable to pick one and prune the other.

Honey mesquite *(Prosopis glandulosa* var. *glandulosa)* and its close relative, **western honey mesquite** *(Prosopis glandulosa* var. *torreyana),* are associated commonly with Texas gardens but do equally well in the Southwest. In my grandparents' Texas backyard, there was a fine old honey mesquite. That tree was a free seedling—no one had planted it—but it was the center of backyard life in my family. Spring was announced each year with the overnight emergence of the tree's distinctive lime-green leaves along its low, sprawling branches. It used to be said by old-timers in that part of Texas that you couldn't count out cold weather until the mesquites had leafed out, and truly they are one of the last species to emerge from winter deciduousness. Mesquites are comfortable trees, at ease and at home in any garden setting—in fact, so fitting that I worry that they will become humdrum and overused.

The honey mesquite is a dark-trunked tree rising to about 30 feet and has distinctive light green leaflets that are larger than those of any other mesquite in horticulture. It has an extensive range in Texas, from the southern tip in the Rio Grande Valley to the plains around Amarillo in the north. Unlike all other mesquites commonly sold, the honey mesquite is completely deciduous throughout the winter.

The differences between the two honey mesquites are subtle. The western honey mesquite has slightly smaller leaflets. The honey mesquite is more cold hardy, tolerating temperatures down to -10°F, while the western honey mesquite remains unharmed down to 10°F.

Screwbean mesquite *(Prosopis pubescens)* is named for its pods, which curl into tight cylinders that are held in snug groups like Christmas ribbon. These pods, like most mesquite pods, are delicious and were highly favored as food by Native American peoples. The screwbean is somewhat smaller than its near relatives, usually 20 feet tall or less, and has a much lighter, more open appearance. Its leaflets are smaller and more sparse than those on the other mesquites. Instead of the wide-spreading crown so common in the larger species, the screwbean mesquite grows into an urnlike form. All of these traits make it a highly suitable choice for smaller, tighter spaces where light shade would be desirable.

Two South American species of mesquite have become popular in desert gardens in recent years: **Chilean mesquite** *(Prosopis chilensis)* and **Argentine mesquite** *(Prosopis alba).* The Chilean mesquite has an upright character, growing to 30 feet or more, and often has a single trunk. The leaflets are fine and straight, and the thorns range from large to virtually invisible. There is at present rampant confusion over just what is a Chilean mesquite. What is called Chilean mesquite in the trade is usually a hybrid between any number of species.

The confusion arose when plants were being selected for their relative thornlessness and it somehow became common to consider the name "Chilean mesquite" as synonymous with a thornless mesquite. Because any mesquite species has thornless individuals, however, the confusion got serious. In addition, mesquites are profligate and hybridize freely, so when seed is collected from areas where more than one species is growing, it is a near certainty the progeny are hybrids. The crazy quilt of plants named Chilean mesquite constitutes the most commonly available forms of mesquite in the region. Despite all the naming chaos, some spectacular individuals have resulted, and unless you must have only thoroughbreds in the garden, buy the plant you like.

The real Chilean mesquite is hardy to about 15°F, and most hybrids have demonstrated at least this much tolerance to cold. Today they are often known simply as South American hybrids, a pedantic but considerably more accurate name for this swarm of excellent plants.

The Argentine mesquite is one of the prettiest mesquites in the trade. A tall, upright tree, it, too, had confusing beginnings. Some of the earliest introductions using this name may have been *Prosopis nigra,* a magnificent close relative. Pure forms of Argentine mesquite have thin leaflets, so that looking up through the tree is like seeing through a glass snow globe overturned above your head. This mesquite attains 30 to 40 feet in height, and although blessed with ferocious white thorns in youth, it loses them fairly quickly on older branches.

All mesquites grow quickly, one of their most valuable assets in horticulture. They can be pushed to grow too quickly, however, and then fall victim to wind early in life. I have seen plantings where more than 90 percent of the trees toppled over within the first two years. There is fierce debate on the cause, but I strongly suspect it has to do with watering. Most are watered frequently to a shallow depth, which produces a puny root system on a large tree. Deeper watering at longer intervals would help alleviate most problems with falling among new plantings.

Palo Verdes

Like their relatives the mesquites, palo verdes are among the most beautiful and water-thrifty trees that can be used in desert gardens. When I look at a palo verde, I marvel at the elegant economy of shifting photosynthesis to the bark in order to save precious water by reducing water loss through leaves. This adaptation not only is effective but has resulted in the extraordinary green bark that makes these plants such wonders in our gardens.

Blue palo verde *(Cercidium floridum)* is a handsome, commanding tree, tall and upright, with a great spreading crown. It shares the distinction of being the state tree of Arizona with the foothills or little-leaf palo verde *(Cercidium microphyllum)*. In nature it rises over washes and drainages, breaking up long, dry plains in the Sonoran Desert. Growing to about 30 feet tall, with a high, spreading crown, the blue palo verde is rapidly becoming a favored plant for street sides and public plantings in Phoenix and Tucson. It is equally at home in large plantings, naturalistic gardens, or as a large shade tree. In early April the blue palo verde leads the cycle of palo verde bloom in the low desert with its intense, bright yellow flowers. The dense bloom lies like a brilliant shawl on the shoulders of the great tree, and as the petals drop to the ground, the yellow drape falls and fades beneath the plant.

Foothills palo verde *(Cercidium microphyllum)* occurs throughout the lower elevations of the Sonoran Desert and is so common that whole hillsides turn green after a rainfall. Shrubby and complicated, the foothills palo verde grows more slowly than most desert trees; some large native individuals are thought to be more than 200 years old. It is superb as a specimen along a complex hedge or row planting or in a naturalistic setting. Each of the branches ends in a thorn, so be careful where you plant this tree. Following its brilliant relative the blue palo verde into bloom, the foothills palo verde has flowers that are a pale, creamy yellow. The pods of all palo verdes are edible, but the tender new pods of the foothills palo verde are especially delicious, raw or steamed.

Palo brea *(Cercidium praecox)* is the stunning Sonoran cousin of the two American palo verdes. This tree is becoming popular, and one look at old trees such as those at the Desert Botanical Garden shows why. The bark, a deep ocean green, is so smooth it resembles a dancer's leotard clinging to the winding branches. About 35 feet tall at maturity, the palo brea has a wide, spreading crown, making it an ideal overhanging shade plant for a patio or yard. It has fewer low branches than other palo verdes, and multitrunked individuals are strong. This sculptural character makes the palo brea an ideal subject for a focal point or a plant to be illuminated in the garden. The palo brea brings on the finale of the palo verde bloom with its brilliant yellow flowers.

None of these species has great cold tolerance, and they are, in fact, severely limited in their range to areas with routine winter temperatures above 22°F.

All palo verdes are susceptible to limb dieback and bark splitting. Limb dieback can result from a number of causes. A common and effective strategy in desert trees is to reduce the number of limbs and leaves that need to be supported in times of drought. When the tree experiences dry soil or endures drought stress for an extended period of time, it begins to lose its outermost branches. For a gardener, dieback is largely a cosmetic concern.

Limbs also can die back as the result of pruning too severely or during cold weather. In this case, the stump will begin to darken and die out, and infection can spread down the limb to adjoining branches. The best treatment is prevention; prune during warm weather, when the plant can heal properly.

Palo verdes have thin bark that can be damaged easily by sharp objects or rough treatment. The palo brea is also particularly susceptible to bark splitting caused by overwatering or by too much water being sprayed on the bark. All these types of wounds are common and usually heal without long-term damage to the tree. Nevertheless, these delicate desert natives require attentive care to keep them in good condition and good health. Infections can be introduced into a tree through wounds or openings, so it is always wise to exercise preventative caution.

Mexican palo verde *(Parkinsonia aculeata)* is a plant with a definite attitude. Fast-growing, rampant in its ability to reseed, it is a bully if you are not careful in choosing its location. Because it is so aggressive, it should never be used anywhere near a park, preserve, or other natural area. Personally, I like the Mexican palo verde, but it is definitely a plant only for the urban core.

The Mexican palo verde is a tall, often graceful tree that bears bright yellow flowers dotted with orange throughout the summer. This species is much more cold hardy than any of the other palo verdes, easily enduring temperatures in the low twenties. Perhaps the best reason to keep the Mexican palo verde around, like a cranky old bull, is that hybrids between it and other palo verdes are often exceptional.

All palo verdes hybridize freely. One hybrid, a complicated three-way cross between foothills palo verde, Mexican palo verde, and blue palo verde, is known as the 'Desert Museum' palo verde. It is a lovely tree that has been out of production for some time but is making a minor comeback. I hope that it returns to our nurseries and gardens. It has a good combination of traits, being more upright and treelike in form than the foothills palo verde, having the green bark characteristic of all palo verdes, and bearing large yellow flowers throughout the summer.

Ironwood

It is fitting that the champion of desert trees, **ironwood** *(Olneya tesota)*, belongs to a monotypic genus. It is truly one of a kind, and what else could even come close to its majesty and beauty? Capable of being a large tree up to 40 feet tall, it grows naturally along washes and is particularly plentiful in the drainages of the western part of Arizona. The pale lavender flowers open after palo verdes bloom, usually in late April and May, looking like a smoky gossamer coating the tree. There is wide color variation in this species; flowers range from pure white to a deep, vivid purple. Like so many desert trees, the ironwood has a complicated multibranching habit, but it develops a single main stem quickly with minor pruning. Interestingly, even old, wild plants eventually shed enough stems to become wonderful shade trees.

The ironwood is long-lived and slow-growing. Mature specimens are hundreds of years old. In the garden an ironwood will grow moderately fast under typical irrigation schedules but rarely bolts with the harelike speed of mesquites or acacias. Tolerant of rocky, dry soils or well-drained wash soils, it is great both for shade and as a screen.

All transplanted trees have, to various degrees, the annoying habit of appearing to sit still after transplant, often fooling the gardener into thinking they are not growing. In fact, that is not true, for during the first year or so after transplant, a tree is busy growing a healthy root system. The ironwood, however, requires even greater patience from the gardener. Often it will barely show any growth for two years or longer, until suddenly one spring it will set new buds and branches. This is the sign that the tree has accepted its new spot and will live there for future generations to enjoy its beauty.

The wood, as indicated by the common name, is very hard; it is heavier than water and does not float. For years in parts of northern Sonora, the wood, which can be worked until it resembles polished stone, was used to make carvings of animals, birds, and plants, which were sold as souvenirs. Sadly, the popularity of this craft led to extreme overharvesting of the trees; now there are sharp restrictions on the use and sale of ironwood wood products.

Acacias

I must confess that although I love its fragrance, I am not altogether fond of **sweet acacia** *(Acacia smallii)* as a shade tree. It is, in my opinion, a difficult and time-consuming tree and without that delicious aroma would not be given room in my garden. I find that the tree is best planted somewhere to the side so that its glorious perfume will waft into bedroom windows or sitting areas.

The best-looking sweet acacias grow in the deeper soils of the West, the interior basins and old drainages between rocky hills, buttes, and mountains. Trees in extremely rocky, poor soils are rarely as vigorous or as large as those grown in deeper soils. They often fail to establish and die slowly within five years of transplant. Sweet acacias planted in deeper soils can grow to be more than 30 feet tall, while those planted in rocky, shallow soils are much smaller.

Sweet acacias, like most desert trees, have a strong multitrunk habit. Judicious and careful pruning when the tree is young, along with consistent removal of suckers, will help maintain the pleasant look and form of the tree. Like mesquites, acacias of all types are prone to growing too far too fast if regularly given too much water. Because a sweet acacia can develop an extremely dense crown, it is wise to prune the crown frequently to keep it open, both for the health of the tree and to prevent serious wind damage. This is achieved by pruning out from the interior and removing the tangle of smaller limbs, downturned branches, and crossing members that fill the space of the tree.

The wood of the sweet acacia is brittle and often splits, particularly if the tree grows too fast. If a broken branch is pruned off, however, the tree generally recovers quickly.

The genus *Acacia* is immense, occurring throughout the subtropical and desert regions of Africa, South America, and Australia. With some practice you can usually judge the origin of a tree by its appearance. African acacias are usually tall and have lusty thorns, small to tiny leaflets, and sometimes beautiful trunks. American acacias are similar but grow more often as shrubs or small trees with good leaf color, less interesting bark, and brighter flowers. Australian acacias characteristically have few true leaves and rely for photosynthesis on phyllodes, which are flattened leaf petioles. They rarely have thorns.

Palo blanco *(Acacia willardiana)* looks like an Australian acacia but hails from Sonora, Mexico. It is a superb tree for small spaces and patios, growing into an airy tree 25 to 30 feet tall. The perfect complement to a well-designed patio, palo blanco is too light to block a view and makes a great frame in a small area. The bark is charming: it is white (hence, the name), and great sheets of it peel off regularly, like the pages of an ancestral scroll, revealing the secrets of the bark beneath.

Twisted acacia *(Acacia schaffneri)* is another wonderful New World acacia that comes and goes in this area; I am told it is hard to propagate. If you find it, you will love it. The branches hold true to their name, winding and swirling with dark, rough bark and dense, green leaves that are clustered on the stem. It is extremely drought tolerant, resistant to the worst soils, and grows to about 20 feet tall, occasionally taller.

I am unduly sentimental about **camelthorn** *(Acacia erioloba),* an African member of the genus, because it was the first species I grew for sale from the Desert Botanical Garden collection. Sentiment aside, I think it is an outstanding member of the suite of tree-form acacias for desert gardens.

Native to the arid plains of southern Africa, the camelthorn is an extremely drought-tolerant species that can soar to 40 feet tall. It makes a stunning tree but needs careful pruning early to encourage a mature tree that will have one or two main trunks. It doesn't take much to get a good straight leader started, but you must work as the giraffe does, nibbling at and shrinking the multiple stems, until the tree grows out to have the distinctive flattened crown so familiar in photographs of the African plains.

Although large by Sonoran tree standards, this beautiful tree is quite compatible with a Sonoran desert garden. The high canopy offers lots of opportunity for planting subtropical desert plants and succulents under its shade and also provides frost protection. The leaflets are dusky gray-green, and the bark light brown, so that the camelthorn blends well with desert gardens and natural areas but provides more height when appropriate. The flowers are creamy white puffballs, followed by gray, flat pods covered with feltlike hairs.

Australian acacias are easy to spot, thanks to their long, prominent phyllodes, which create the weeping, lazy form for which they are highly prized. **Blue-leaf wattle** *(Acacia saligna),* **willow acacia** *(Acacia salicina),* and **shoestring acacia** *(Acacia stenophylla)* are the most common in the Phoenix area. All are quite drought tolerant, responding well to dry, well-drained soils and irregular deep irrigation. They give a garden a more lush, tropical look because of their larger leaves. Blue-leaf wattle and willow acacia grow to about 30 feet and spread almost that wide. Shoestring acacia, as the name implies, is much leaner, growing to 30 feet but with a more columnar growth habit.

Leather-leaf acacia *(Acacia craspedocarpa)* is an odd small tree. Its small leaves are leathery, as the tree's name suggests, and have a distinctive light tan to green hue. The entire tree is usually 15 to 20 feet tall and dense. The close-set leaves and shrublike form make it an excellent choice for a background or against a boring wall. This tree is tough, requires full sun for best growth and form, and is extremely drought tolerant once established.

Acacia peuce is something of a curiosity plant. With stiff, branchlike phyllodes, the species strongly resembles the Sonoran native graythorn *(Zizyphus obtusifolia)*. It has a striking blue-gray color in older age and retains a tall, thin, weeping appearance, which when coupled with the stark thorns, is vivid and unusual.

More Tree Choices

Texas ebony *(Pithecellobium flexicaule)* is a dark, brooding tree from southern Texas and adjacent Mexico, dissimilar in appearance to most desert trees. Evergreen (which means that it loses its leaves a few at a time rather than all at once) and rarely more than 20 feet tall, this is a splendid tree for a small area. The crown spreads just enough to offer respite from the grueling desert sun, and the powdery white flowers are fragrant. The entire genus is characterized by stems that angle and turn in a zigzag pattern. The dense, complicated crown of the Texas ebony, coupled with its dark green leaflets, makes it a good choice for a screen or to hide an unsightly view.

There is a house in Phoenix where a row of Texas ebonies were planted, probably over 20 years ago, at the edge of the street. Having never been pruned, they formed an impenetrable hedge offering great privacy and noise control. Where I was raised, it would have been called a hog fence, and it would have worked.

A near relative, **palo chino** *(Pithecellobium mexicanum)*, also called Mexican ebony, is little seen but deserves to be more widely grown. Cold deciduous and with light gray-green leaves, this tree has a lighter, more open crown than Texas ebony but retains the complex branching so typical of this genus. It is also a taller tree, growing up to 30 feet, and its height and form make it more suitable as the principal shade tree in a yard or patio. The cream-colored powder-puff flowers are lightly fragrant.

My favorite of this genus is the seldom seen **tenaza** *(Pithecellobium pallens)*. It is a reasonably small tree, usually only up to 15 feet tall, with exquisitely fragrant flowers that occur erratically throughout the summer. The small white flowers are prolific, and when touched by the last rays of sundown, the tree glows as if it were covered with a thousand small lights.

I have planted a pair at the base of a small stairway in the hope of creating a scented gateway to the vegetable garden. The fragrance is glorious, a lingering sweet vanilla mixed with something sharp and clean; this trait alone makes the tenaza a most desirable tree. It has small, fine, green-gray leaflets held on the contorted branches so pronounced in this genus. This tree is ideal for a small patio or courtyard. It is a collector's plant now but should be more widely known and grown.

There are other delightful members of the genus *Pithecellobium*, but they suffer from the stigma of being cold sensitive. Whether they are or not is subject to good testing, but **guamúchil** *(Pithecellobium dulce)* and *Pithecellobium confine* deserve more attention and trials, particularly in the warmer parts of the Southwest.

The first **desert willow** *(Chilopsis linearis)* that I saw surprised me; I could not believe it was a desert species. A light tree with long thin leaves in summer, it is crowded with large orchid-colored flowers from late spring through summer. It is softer and more lush looking than most desert trees. Where I found it revealed a lot about how tough this tree is; it was growing along an abandoned road and received only incidental irrigation from a garden on the other side of a wall. I soon found out that the size of the tree depends entirely on how much water is available; massive specimens grow along the Salt and other rivers in Arizona.

Flowers are exquisite little trumpets that range in color from a pale mauve to a vivid deep purple. It is no wonder that a number of cultivars have been recently showing up in nurseries. Dark colors, ruffled edges, multitoned, pure white or pure purple, the combinations are countless and all worth exploring. Few of the named cultivars are grown in the desert at this time, but it won't be long until we see them all. Because there is so much variation and most cultivars are fairly recent, it is smart to see the plant in bloom before you buy it.

The desert willow fits in with most plantings, but it looks particularly fine as the anchor of a large perennial planting or rising over a nice wall. It can look extremely lush, almost tropical, in the garden, but it is deciduous. You may want to place it toward the back of a bed or planting when summer color is the main reason for having it around.

When I murdered my camelthorn, it was a **lysiloma** *(Lysiloma watsonii,* formerly *Lysiloma thornberi)* that replaced it. I have taken to calling it lysiloma as a common name, much as we say salvia or penstemon, because I think fern-of-the-desert not only is an awkward mouthful of words but is an oxymoronic way to describe a plant, sort of like "pond prickly pear." It is a common name that just doesn't work for me.

The lysiloma reminds me of the yellow car axiom: When you covet something—a yellow car, earrings that talk, or a special tree—you think it unique. You find out when you own it that the object of your desire is extremely common; you just hadn't noticed it. Before planting that lysiloma, I thought of it as an underused species, but both street-side and public plantings of this lovely tree are common, I now realize to my personal delight.

The lysiloma is tough, accepting of sun and poor soils. Drought tolerant when established but with a deceptive soft, lacy look, it is an ideal plant for smoothing and softening any hot or severe location. It fits in almost anywhere and is a superior choice for areas where you might think of putting a mimosa, a plant that struggles in the alkaline soils of the desert. Usually about 20 feet tall, lysilomas often have multiple trunks that can be persuaded into living sculpture in the garden.

A rarely seen Sonoran relative, **palo blanco** *(Lysiloma candida)*, has graced the Desert Botanical Garden as long as I can remember. Before the Webster complex was renovated in 1989, it stood in a planter outside the back entrance to the auditorium. This was near my office at the time, and I came to admire greatly the white-gray mottled bark and the cream-colored flowers floating over its branches. It was boxed and relocated to Ullmann Terrace when the renovation was complete, and although it had a rough time adjusting, it is now the star of the terrace.

Young plants of palo blanco can be quite cold tender, which is one reason it is hard to find. It grows fast and straight, however, into a tree usually 30 to 40 feet tall. It is extremely drought tolerant when established.

As long as I am going on about underused species, let me speak in favor of **kidneywood** *(Eysenhardtia orthocarpa)* and its close relative **Texas kidneywood** *(Eysenhardtia texana)*. These lovely, delicate trees have a place in smaller areas. Their flowers are fragrant and spicy, with just a hint of vanilla, intoxicating on a warm summer night. The fruit occurs as flattened pods clustered into small straw-colored pagodas on the plant and is nearly as attractive as the tiny white flowers.

Cascalote *(Caesalpinia cacalaco)* is a relative newcomer to horticulture in the Southwest. Although long held in a number of botanical garden collections, it is just now emerging as a well-used ornamental. A native of northwestern Mexico, this medium-sized flowering tree has dark green circular leaflets and reddish brown thorns similar to those found on roses. Young plants are multitrunked shrubs and can be thorny. With careful pruning, the cascalote forms a graceful tree, and as it ages, the thorns widen to become woody and eventually fall off. Plants flower young, often while still in a container.

The cascalote will reach 25 feet in height and has a moderate growth rate. It is a good choice for a patio or seating area, providing dense enough shade to relieve the summer heat but broken enough to provide excellent cover for smaller plants. Flowering begins in December with great 2-foot, narrow spikes of clear yellow flowers. Seen from a distance, the tree appears to be decorated with curving yellow candles. On closer inspection, the flowers are tight and waxy, with a bright red spot on one of the yellow petals. I am fond of this tree and think of it as a hallmark of the winter season.

Quite drought tolerant when established, the cascalote looks better and blooms better if given regular deep irrigation in the hottest part of the summer. Under deep stress it will begin to lose leaves and occasionally branches will die back, but a good deep watering will soon put it back on track.

Mexican bird of paradise *(Caesalpinia mexicana)* is a summer blooming shrub or tree. In fact, it can grow to 20 feet tall or more and makes an extremely handsome small tree. It blooms regularly and continuously throughout the warm season, bearing bright yellow flowers that contrast its dark green leaves. Like the cascalote, it has good drought tolerance but will thrive with additional water.

An uncommon relative, *Caesalpinia platyloba,* is a fine small tree for the low desert region. Rarely more than 20 feet tall, it is an open tree with large round leaflets. The small yellow flowers are unremarkable, appearing in late summer, but the leaves turn a warm copper red in the early winter.

Smoketree *(Psorothamnus spinosus,* formerly *Dalea spinosa)* can be found in the western parts of Arizona and the Coachella Valley of California, but it remains uncommon horticulturally. It is an exquisite tree, a floating vision of gray and white most of the year. But in the late spring, flowers of an impossibly dense, dark indigo cover the plant briefly before it retires into its leafless, ghost-white repose for the summer. A denizen of desert washes, the plant can take infrequent irrigation during the summer but demands sharp drainage.

One reason smoketree has been hard to find is that it can be tricky to transplant. It likes to be moved when it is warm, even hot, and it thrives on plenty of water when transplanted. Although not well tested in cooler climates, it is likely not to be hardy out of the low desert.

Golden ball lead tree *(Leucaena retusa),* a tree that definitely needs a new common name, is native to western Texas and northern Mexico. Usually left to grow as a loose shrub, it is nevertheless stunning when pruned into a small tree. The flowers are brilliant, lustrous golden balls, large and profuse. Against the tree's dark green leaflets, the contrast is exquisite. Cold hardy for the lower desert region, golden ball lead tree can tolerate temperatures down to 15°F.

Another lovely smaller tree is **brasilwood** *(Haematoxylon brasiletto).* Its torturous botanical name derives from the fact that the sap is blood red *(haemato)* and is used as a dye. Native to Sonora, the brasilwood blooms in the spring with light yellow flowers followed by equally attractive pink pods. The pods hold on a long time, waiting to be set afire by the setting autumnal sun.

The brasilwood begins, like so many desert legumes, as a multitrunked complicated bush. Pruning to bring out a single trunk is easy, and because the plant is fast growing, a small tree emerges quickly. The brasilwood grows rapidly during late summer, when the humidity is high and the heat intense. In nature it is deciduous in the early, dry summer but with irrigation will hold its leaves through midsummer. In the Phoenix area plants can be damaged by temperatures in the midtwenties but recover quickly. In the Tucson area and higher elevations, this species needs winter protection.

Rhus is a genus usually associated with shrubs, but in Africa a suite of species readily grow to be trees. The one most familiar to low desert gardeners is **African sumac** *(Rhus lancea),* a difficult and messy tree. Although highly drought tolerant, this is a plant that requires careful placement and should never be used outside the deep urban core. It reseeds plentifully but can work well in the right circumstances.

The African sumac grows a profusion of stems that strike out in every direction—to many an annoying habit. However, I am fond of those complicated branches, which create an unusual and distinctive form, yet I cannot deny it takes diligent and attentive pruning to keep the tree looking its best.

When we moved into our present house, a mature African sumac was growing with more stems than a tree actually needs. It required three years of careful pruning to clear out the mess, but it was worth it; the tree is now a fine specimen gently protecting an aloe and succulent garden from too much sun and cold.

The African sumac is generally considered a messy tree, and if it is placed over a pool, I would agree. But all that litter can be useful in the right place by increasing organic matter in the soil and building a nice, rich bed underneath the tree.

I am intrigued by desert pines, perhaps because pines are fixed in my mind as species of the mountains and high-elevation canyons, where the air is cool and their scent is fresh and the faint whistle of wind in their needles exhilarating. But there really are desert pines, and **Aleppo pine** *(Pinus halepensis)* is one of the most drought tolerant and alkaline soil resistant of them all. As its name suggests, the Aleppo pine is from Syria and Iran, an area of the Middle East that is almost exactly analogous to the lower Sonoran Desert of Arizona.

The only problem that I have with this species is that it can become enormous and bury the house, the yard, and the street where it is planted. Aleppo pines can rise to 60 feet tall and in regularly irrigated areas create a thundercloud of a canopy. Used more wisely, where it fits the size of the garden and is not overwatered, this hardy pine can be a good choice for a large garden, providing thick shade and excellent frost protection beneath its boughs.

I must admit that I am stubbornly resistant to the charms of **eucalyptus.** My attitude is not entirely rational—I just don't care for them. Most of my distaste arises from the fact that most of the eucalyptus in common use here are huge, great, hulking things that might work on a fairway-sized property but rarely succeed in a common urban setting. My neighborhood, though remarkable for all the native vegetation left untouched 40 years ago when it was developed, has houses with a great eucalyptus in the yard. I would live in eternal fear of the thing crashing down on me at any time.

Although not all eucalyptus are brittle, white ironbark *(Eucalyptus leucoxylon)* and flooded gum *(Eucalyptus rudis)* are notorious for their ability to shatter and flail limbs about. Many of these large trees are drought tolerant, but they are highly susceptible to chlorosis when overwatered, and on a well-watered lawn or golf course, the poor things always look a little pathetic.

In a genus of more than 500 species, all woody, it is a wonder that species with more congenial size and form have not been introduced into desert gardens. When that happens, perhaps I will drop my reluctance and accept eucalyptus as worthy garden plants, but not, I am fairly sure, within my own garden.

3 Desert Palms

Palms are so evocative of beaches and the luxuriant flora of the tropics that it is sometimes difficult to remember that a significant number of palms are native to the deserts and semiarid regions of the world. Arizona, in fact, boasts one native palm, the desert fan palm, often sold as California fan palm. The closely related Mexican fan palm is native to the deserts of Baja California. There are a couple of dozen species of palms native to the arid regions of Mexico, Africa, Australia, and the Middle East. A number of palms are from seasonally wet and dry areas, a heritage that makes them suitable for gardening in the low desert.

In desert or arid regions, palms are often the denizens of oases, canyons, and other places that collect water or have a shallow water table. In the driest parts of Arizona, California, and Mexico, palms often cluster at fault lines that permit the upwelling of groundwater, such as the springs at Anza Borrego and Coachella Springs in California and Desert Hot Springs in Arizona. Although they occur in such benign natural conditions, desert palms are remarkably drought tolerant in ornamental settings and are certainly well suited to the soils and intense sunshine of the low desert regions.

This does not mean that palms are appropriate for every garden and situation. Some can grow to extraordinary heights, making them unsuitable for the small garden. Most palms develop their crown to full size early, while it is still near ground level. As the trunk grows and matures, it raises the great crown like a glorious tent. Therefore the tree needs ample space to accommodate the crown during its growth.

All palms are best planted when the weather is warm, even hot. They are nearly guaranteed to fail when planted in cool soil. It is important to give them a deep soaking twice a week during their first summer. As they grow older, less frequent watering, two deep soakings per month, is adequate and will control the rate of their growth.

Palms have few pests, although some species are susceptible to a bewildering fungal infection known as crown rot, which usually occurs among large, older plants. The entire crown of leaves begins to look languid, and then the leaves wilt and fall until finally only the central bud remains upright, a clear sign of this generally lethal infection. If the palm is small, a good fungicide bath in the crown will help, but little can be done to save large plants.

Palm Choices...

The **desert fan palm** *(Washingtonia filifera)* and **Mexican fan palm** *(Washingtonia robusta)* are extremely tall, growing to 50 feet or more; very old Mexican fan palms can exceed 80 feet in height, earning them the lyric name skyduster but making them a problem for most small yards. These trees should be placed where they are visible in the distance or planted at the bottom of a wash or canyon so that one views their tops. I think they look best planted in groups, crowded and crammed together in a dozen different sizes, hard fans whistling in the light desert breeze, tops full of birds.

Both of these species are rigorously pruned, a practice of dubious aesthetic or cultural value. Both species, but particularly the desert fan palm, will hold their old leaves long after the death of the leaf, creating a great skirt all the way to the ground. The cluster of dead leaves can be a fire hazard and insect lure, but removing them from the lower 15 to 20 feet minimizes such problems. Old, tall fan palms are pruned by the intense monsoon winds, which rip off all but the living leaves.

Mexican blue palm or hesper palm *(Brahea armata)* is probably the prettiest of the desert palms. A Sonoran native, it is slow growing and takes a generation to reach its ultimate height of 40 feet. Even young plants are graced with the wide gray-blue fan leaves that give the tree its name. This is a terrific pool and patio plant, both for its great beauty and for its dense head, which occurs at a manageable height. Cream-colored flowers emerge on a stalk that bends out and over the head until it nearly touches the ground.

A couple of close relatives, also from Mexico, are not used as commonly. *Brahea edulis* is greener but of the same proportions as the Mexican blue palm. Both species are tolerant of cold to 20°F and can be used throughout the low desert region. *Brahea brandegeei* is a green-leaved palm growing much taller than the other two species. It is more cold sensitive, surviving without damage down to only 25°F.

Mexico is also home to the desert members of the genus *Sabal*. This is the genus of the cabbage palms of Florida and countless other Caribbean basin members. They are characterized by the graceful arch of the costapalmate leaves, which are large and fan shaped and moderate in size. *Sabal uresana* has a blue-green leaf, while the leaf of *Sabal texana* is a dark green. Both species are cold tolerant and work well as a lush backdrop or frame. They are much smaller trees than the ubiquitous desert fan palm and the date palms.

Canary Island date palm (Phoenix canariensis) *GARY IRISH*

Palms from desert regions are well adapted to the alkalinity of desert soils. A number of palms are not, however, most notably **queen palm** *(Syagrus romanzoffiana)*. Many, if not most, of these plants frequently display iron chlorosis, making them one of the most dramatic failures in palm plantings in low desert regions. Queen palms suffer from extreme heat, as well as alkaline soils. This combination of stressful growing conditions results in poor leaf color, poor growth, and short lives for these plants. While queen palms are exquisite when grown in coastal California, most look as if they should have been reconsidered in desert cities.

Species in the genus *Livistona* are characterized by large fan-shaped leaves and drooping leaf tips. All of them work well in the garden as screens or backdrops. The most commonly available species, **Chinese fan palm** *(Livistona chinensis)*, grows best in shaded, protected areas. *Livistona decipiens* and *Livistona australis* are more heat and drought tolerant but much harder to find.

Australian deserts are home to the extremely drought-tolerant *Livistona mariae*. This lovely fan palm has dramatically red juvenile foliage. Growing slowly to 30 feet tall, this fan palm makes a good shelter, screening, or accent plant in the desert garden. It is not commonly available but well worth growing if you find it.

The oldest desert cultures in the world, those from the Middle East, have nurtured and been nurtured by one palm species throughout history. The **date palm** *(Phoenix dactylifera)* has been grown in association with humans in oases for so long that there are no longer wild populations outside these narrow limits. Archaeological evidence of their ancient cultivation abounds. A grove of these plants, tall and often multitrunked, with long pinnate leaves, creates exquisite light shade. Anything will thrive and grow beneath it.

Date palms were brought to the Phoenix area around the beginning of the twentieth century as an agricultural crop. Old groves of large individuals can still be seen around town. The gray-green leaves contrast with the tall, straight trunk. Numerous suckers occur in some individuals and may be removed and rooted to make a new plant.

Birds adore the ripening dates, so protect the fruit by covering it with cloth or sacking until ripe. Treat yourself to a fresh date at least once in your life; it is a delicious fruit, refreshing and filling at the same time. If you are not interested in harvesting the fruit, cut the bloom stalk as soon as it has bloomed out or leave it for the birds.

There are other members of the genus *Phoenix* that do well in low desert conditions. **Canary Island date palm** *(Phoenix canariensis)* is one, but it needs plenty of room. Its enormous head of fronds can reach a diameter of 25 feet,

Mexican blue palm (Brahea armata) **MARY IRISH**

and the tree will ultimately be 50 feet tall, sometimes taller. This is an excellent plant to fill a corner of a large lot, but it should be sited carefully because of its size.

An interesting diamond pattern is created on the large trunks of Canary Island date palms by the petioles left behind as leaves are pruned away. The trunk of a young tree is wider at the base than at the top, and because of this crisscross pattern, it looks like a gigantic pineapple.

Senegal date palm *(Phoenix reclinata)* is a more refined, delicate member of this genus. This palm is usually multitrunked but can be pruned from a young age to as many or as few trunks as desired. Graceful deep green, arching leaves top the plant, which is probably underutilized as a border or screening plant.

Pygmy date palm *(Phoenix roebelenii)* is one of the best poolside plants for the desert garden. Rarely growing more than 10 feet tall, it has numerous fine, smooth leaves that droop gracefully from the crown with a soft, cooling appearance. The pygmy date palm grows best with its feet in good, enriched soil, with its leaves in full sun, and with regular summer irrigation. Plants do well in large planters or a pot.

There are some other unexpectedly good palms for the desert. **Mediterranean fan palm** *(Chamaerops humilis)* is a slow-growing dark-leaved palm with hundreds of stems. Left unpruned, these stems shoot out symmetrically from the plant to form an impenetrable ball. Pruned to fewer stems early in its development, however, the plant grows into a formal symmetry. Mediterranean in origin, it tolerates the alkaline soils, high heat, and dry air of the low desert. Regular summer irrigation promotes good growth and good health in this species.

Bamboo palms *(Chamaedorea* spp.) are a large group of tropical palms, mostly from the rain forests of Central America and Asia. Despite its origins, *Chamaedorea seifrizii* does extremely well outdoors in the low desert, growing to more than 8 feet in height and bearing hundreds of individual stems. Like the pygmy date palm, this palm prefers its feet in good, enriched soil, its head in the sun, and regular irrigation.

A common theme in desert gardening links palms to lawns and lakes. It is our mental association that has brought them together, because palms have no more natural affinity for lawns than cacti do. I am impatient with this demonization of palms, particularly because they are in many ways the very symbol of desert life, a source of shelter, food, and fiber for desert peoples over the millennia. Rather than reviling palms, I would prefer they be appreciated, as all good plants should be, through wise use in desert gardens.

Many desert gardeners suffer great ambivalence about palm trees. A dear friend who was transforming his front yard from a boring lawn with a few languishing shrubs to one rich in native species was greatly disturbed to learn that two desert fan palms were native. He left them, mostly because of the trouble and expense it would take to remove them, but he could not reconcile those palms with his idea of a desert garden. One day years later, as we were examining an old garden that the owner wanted us to revive, my friend looked up into the ancient face of a small group of date palms. He said they were beautiful, so beautiful, he would have one if he could. I knew then that he was looking at the very heart of a desert garden and the plants that can make it possible.

4 Shrubs

*T*hey are everywhere, yet we never notice them. Mentally erase all the shrubs on street medians, in your yard, throughout parking lots, or around a park, and you get an idea of how commonplace shrubs are in our lives. Shrubs provide the framework of a garden. They are the walls of a garden's house, the bones of a garden's being. The entire spirit or purpose of a garden is defined by the shrubs that are planted in it.

Desert gardens in particular benefit from a bounty of shrubs from the desert flora of the world. Woody plants, large and small, are one of the largest group of plants found in desert regions. There are light ones and dark ones, those with long blooming displays and others with little bloom, some with showy fruit and others with tiny, innocuous fruit. Desert shrubs range from large and dense to small and airy, and nothing ought to restrain us from using a wide selection of them.

In gardening, *shrub* is not a well-defined term. This book regards shrubs as woody plants that are fairly large, at least 4 feet in height and often taller but not more than about 12 feet tall. Although shrubs can easily be pruned into a small single-trunked tree, they naturally exhibit a complicated multibranching habit, and that is what makes them shrubs. So while a foothills palo verde is a complicated multibranched plant, it is too big for me to call a shrub. And while brittlebush develops a woody base, it is too small for me to call a shrub.

Shrubs in the Garden...

Shrubs have many uses in the garden. With clever placement and sufficient size or density, shrubs can hide horrid buildings, piles of junk, or a neighbor's unsightly mistakes. In a place with lots of room, shrubs like desert hackberry or rosewood can be coupled with unpruned mesquites or palo verdes to hide anything. In smaller gardens or amid smaller affronts, Texas ranger, jojoba, desert persimmon, or Texas olive will achieve the same results.

Shrubs are often used to soften a hard edge or wall or to define and frame a great view. For this use it is harder to generalize about which shrubs might be suitable; the choices should be dictated by the style and scale of the garden.

Shrubs commonly serve as a backdrop of gentle shape and color, giving depth and substance to more dramatic or busy plantings. Shrubs for this purpose can be bland, offering only a background; Arizona rosewood, jojoba, or desert barberry fit this use well. Background shrubs, however, may serve a more important role in the overall scheme by providing color or texture that enhances or repeats various parts of the garden. In this case, selection depends on the look or style of the whole planting; evergreen shrubs such as 'Pink Beauty', copper-leaved caesalpinia, or shrubby senna are good examples of shrubs with strong seasonal color.

An ancient tradition is to use shrubs to create boundaries or divisions. At the time of the Norman Conquest of England, the Saxons were delineating garden plots through the use of a *haga,* a pocket of sticks and poles filled with thorny twigs and branches. Barriers like this are self-perpetuating; as birds use them, seed is deposited, and the resulting hedge continues virtually forever. These plantings formed the origin of English hedgerows, some of which still stand.

Hedges have long served as living boundaries and as bird and animal refuges where land is intensively cultivated or developed. Without the room necessary for large hedges, American suburban gardeners remain dedicated to formal, uniform plantings on lot borders to separate one garden from another. The use of smaller plants, however, might save some neighborhoods from being overwhelmed by their hedges.

Generally, a hedge is uniform, a long and uninterrupted line of one species. This type of planting is very effective in drawing your eye down the line of hedge, but hedges can achieve a richer, more interesting vista if a combination of species is used. This type of planting is known as a tapestry hedge. I am fond of this concept and have been trying to find a good spot to try one. Tightly planted desert sumac, Texas ranger, quail bush, and barberry would be an interesting combination. Each blooms at a different time, has variously colored fruit, and both the desert sumac and the barberry have striking foliage. These characteristics would result in a hedge with year-round interest.

Equally ancient traditions of plant boundaries have come to us from the Middle East, where hedges evolved into walls of myrtle *(Myrtus communis),* laurel *(Laurus nobilis),* or jasmine *(Jasminum* spp.) to serve as a backdrop for more colorful species. These plant walls did not define property boundaries but garden boundaries, separating various areas or lining walkways between garden rooms. From this style came the exquisite formal gardens of Italy and later France, where the form and texture of large woody shrubs and trees were exaggerated and refined to provide crisp, stylized gardens.

A great desert garden shaped by desert shrubs is enhanced by the addition of yuccas, agaves, and other rosette succulents. Instead of color, such a garden would emphasize textural contrast and the assorted leaf colors of these plants. Here in the desert Southwest, the comfortable informality of a naturalistic style works well in most gardens, but there is always room for experimentation.

Shrubs provide excellent food and shelter for wildlife, and a good selection of shrubs will rapidly transform a barren, birdless yard into a wildlife sanctuary. Species such as hackberry, desert sumac, creosote, barberry, and graythorn offer a bounty of the berries craved by thrashers, towhees, mockingbirds, and phoebes. Dense shrubbery, such as Texas ranger, rosewood, and jojoba, provide cover for nests for a wide range of birds, both in the boughs and on the ground beneath.

Planting and Watering...

Desert shrubs are among the most carefree and effortless plantings in a garden. Like trees, woody shrubs are best planted in the fall, although spring planting works if regular watering is provided throughout the first summer. Dig holes and plant the same way as for trees, and remember that all shrubs need to be watered thoroughly and deeply in warm weather.

As desert woody shrubs mature, they need much less frequent watering, doing best with heavy, deep soaks at long intervals. Shrubs can yellow, weaken, or develop root rot if they are watered, even in maturity, by sprinkler systems that deliver a light watering three to five times a week. Once they are well established, most shrubs, including all desert shrubs, do better with weekly watering that lasts two hours or longer, depending on the size of the plant and the condition of the soil. It is wise to carefully monitor the watering of shrubs during the summer thunderstorm season, which is when most root rot infections break out.

Pruning...

The pruning of shrubs arouses contentious debate in gardening and landscape maintenance circles. Formal pruning, whether to form crisp boxes, rounded shapes, or mannerly hedges, can be exquisite in a garden with the structure and the size to accommodate it. Too often, however, such clipping is done just for its own sake, without regard for whether the style fits the garden. I am never drawn to plants with a "poodle cut" or "lollipop" pruning; such conceits are rarely successful and most of the time are entirely useless. It is a lot of work to keep a formally pruned garden plant in shape, and because desert shrubs have such lovely form and so much natural symmetry, rigorous pruning seems an unnecessary extravagance.

Texas ranger (Leucophyllum frutescens *'White Cloud'*) **GARY IRISH**

Pruning on a schedule is even worse. Most desert shrubs need only occasional clipping to remove deadwood or bring down their size. Pruning by the calendar not only reduces the vigor of the plant but frequently causes a loss of good bloom. There are good and bad times to prune, and they vary for different species. Severe shearing repeated often throughout a season increases heat stress on the plants, makes them vulnerable to disease and deformity, and results in a shorter life.

Pruning should be an occasional thing: taking out deadwood, gently molding and shaping a plant to enhance its natural form, working with the plant rather than against it. Selected stems and branches should be taken out near the main stem as health and shaping demand. The exception is pruning for a hedge. Because good hedge plants are usually dense, with a complex pattern of stem growth, a formal hedge will not reach desired fullness without the rigors of regular pruning.

I am convinced that pruning cannot be performed satisfactorily with power tools. The best pruning is done from the inside out, taking out a limb here and there. Good hand pruners and a lopper are the tools of choice.

As a rule, fast-growing species present a problem when used as a hedge. They must be pruned constantly to keep them in shape or scale. Slower-growing species, such as Texas ranger, rosewood, jojoba, or barberry, need less pruning and create less litter. In addition, slower-growing species hold and maintain their shape longer.

Shrub Choices...

Leucophyllum

I was raised in Texas, but I am eternally perplexed that most people assume I have an affinity for anything that comes from that state. I do find, however, that species from the Chihuahuan Desert areas of Texas are some of the most interesting and useful shrubs for the desert garden. By anyone's reckoning, plants in the genus *Leucophyllum*, variously known as Chihuahuan sage, Texas ranger, or Texas sage, are superb shrubs for the low desert. In fact, Texas rangers have taken this region by storm. Most of the types in use today are the result of selections made by the late Bennie Simpson and Lynn Lowery, among others.

Texas rangers are extremely frost hardy; most species are undamaged down to 10°F. All species grow in wonderful graceful forms; they never need aggressive pruning because of the nearly perfect shape they achieve on their own. Amazingly, these plants will accept severe shearing, but I think plants pruned drastically generally look insipid.

Texas ranger *(Leucophyllum frutescens)* is the species from which the 'Cloud' cultivars of shrubs are derived. A common shrub in West Texas and throughout eastern Mexico, it is big, often growing up to 8 feet tall and spreading 4 to 6 feet. The gray-green foliage is small and held tightly on the plant. The flowers range from a light pink or mauve to an intense magenta and are covered with fine hairs that give them a soft, fuzzy appearance. The flowers are lightly fragrant, and a large group of plants can create a gentle aroma.

The plants bloom so regularly in response to summer rain that in Texas they are known as barometer bush. They can be counted on to bloom about 10 days after a good summer rain and irregularly after a long irrigation. Occasionally they will bloom in the spring when late spring rains occur.

Texas rangers are carefree shrubs; old ones are often seen in abandoned or neglected yards. They are best watered sparingly in the summer, as they are extremely susceptible to root rot at that time. This can be a problem in clay soils, but with careful watering, this shrub can be grown almost anywhere.

Three cultivars from *Leucophyllum frutescens* are common in the trade. 'Green Cloud', as the name implies, has green foliage with dark magenta flowers. This cultivar is large, 6 to 8 feet tall and not quite that large around. 'White Cloud' is usually not quite as large, growing up to 5 or 6 feet tall, and bears pure white flowers. 'Compacta' is supposedly smaller, although it is hard to tell most of the time. It is slightly more compact, owing to a shorter space between the internodes (the little junctions where leaves arise from the stem are nodes, so internodes are the spaces in between), and its blooms are a light purple.

One of the most handsome of all the Texas rangers in cultivation is the species *Leucophyllum candidum*. It is large, with plants easily reaching 8 feet in height, but the foliage is light, in some individuals a bright, electric white. The flower color is intense, a dense, brooding purple so dark it is sinister. The contrast between leaf and flower color is both startling and dazzling.

The cultivar 'Silver Cloud' was chosen for its white foliage and deep purple flowers. The cultivar 'Thunder Cloud' has dark purple flowers that are prolific and dense, held close to the stem. This gives the plant the appearance of being nothing but flowers when it is in bloom, a glorious sight when it is planted in mass. 'Thunder Cloud' is not large, generally 4 feet tall and about 3 feet wide.

Chihuahuan sage *(Leucophyllum laevigatum)* is a lighter version of the two previously described members of the genus. Its green leaves are quite small and sparse, giving the shrub a lighter, more open appearance. In addition, Chihuahuan sage is about 4 feet tall and just as wide, further exaggerating its open look. Lovely dark lavender flowers appear in late summer.

Leucophyllum zygophyllum is seen less often, and that is a shame because it is a wonder. Usually shrubs are less than 4 feet tall, with foliage that is tan to white and flowers of an extraordinarily deep, dark purple. It is a stunning plant and looks remote and formal.

Leucophyllum pruinosum is the most fragrant species currently in cultivation. A large shrub, up to 6 feet tall, it has pale gray-green to green leaves. Its flowers are lavender with a pale underside, and their fragrance will fill a yard, especially because the shrub blooms when the weather is humid.

Leucophyllum langmaniae is a large shrub, growing to 6 feet or taller, with dark green foliage. Its flowers are blue to violet and appear in late summer or fall.

There are a number of hybrids around. 'Rain Cloud', a hybrid between *Leucophyllum frutescens* and *Leucophyllum minus*, has a more vertical habit than most of the species; it grows to 4 to 6 feet tall. The flowers are dark purple on gray foliage. 'Heavenly Cloud' is thought to be a hybrid of *Leucophyllum laevigatum* and *Leucophyllum candidum* 'Silver Cloud'. This chance seedling has dense, dark green foliage covered with deep indigo flowers. It is a heavy bloomer and repeats blooming over the summer. 'Convent' is a plant whose origins I have not been able to trace satisfactorily. It came to me from a Texas grower but is not in common commerce there or in Arizona. It is nevertheless a lovely shrub that blooms pink with lots of blue undertones, colors that contrast beautifully with the gray foliage. This plant is not widely grown currently but should be; the color combination is different from that of most Texas rangers and increases the range of uses for the group.

Leucophyllum revolutum has recently appeared on the scene, but frankly I am not much taken with it except as a novelty. It looks nothing like the other leucophyllums: quite upright, with small, close-set, narrow leaves, the plant resembles a bottle bush. It does, however, have the great purple flowers so revered in this group.

Creosote

Almost any American desert scene includes **creosote** *(Larrea tridentata)*. This essential desert shrub is at home in the cold Chihuahuan foothills, along the murderous arid flats of the lower Sonoran zone of southern Arizona, and in the great sand dunes of the Colorado River plains.

My own yard and most of my neighborhood is replete with mature creosotes. This is sadly becoming rarer, even in areas where creosote naturally occurs densely; builders seldom leave it in place. And although creosote is much more commonly grown and available than it used to be, it is still treated as a novelty rather than the basic foundation plant of a desert garden. In the

Phoenix and Tucson areas, great trouble and expense are used to spare gigantic old cacti and trees, but that same care is rarely expended on mature creosotes.

I consider creosote to be the basis of a great desert garden. No other species so encapsulates the region; delicate and graceful in form, it is a shrub of nearly unrivaled suitability for arid conditions. Desert gardens without creosote look incomplete, especially those that strive to be naturalistic in their design. Something is missing, a uniting force in the garden. A garden without creosote is adequate but not inspired; it will be a reflection of the desert but not show its full, lively countenance.

The species known botanically as *Larrea tridentata* (and erroneously as *Larrea divaricata*) gained its common name from the similarity of its smell to the wood tar product creosote. There is no connection, but the smell of creosote on a humid day, after a heavy dew, or on a warm morning following a nighttime summer thunderstorm is sharp and cleansing, invigorating to the senses.

Creosote is one of the finest garden plants for attracting and maintaining a steady troop of wildlife. Verdins in particular feed voraciously on the fruit; house finches devour the flowers; and thrashers, quail, towhees, and wrens rifle through the leaf litter for bugs and small worms.

While creosote is extremely drought tolerant, with a steady supply of water and excellent drainage, it will grow to extreme size and retain its dark, dense green leaves throughout the year. One in my backyard is immense. I could not understand its unnatural size and breadth until work on the septic system revealed that it had been growing adjacent to the leach field. This hulking giant has had an entire bed and a patio built to accentuate its huge, sheltering limbs. Over the years tiny cacti, robust succulents, and unusual plants that need just a little break from the sun have nestled under its branches.

Creosote looks unlike most shrubs. Because it is light and open, it provides the perfect shade for smaller plants, particularly cacti and succulents, offering just enough of a break from the harsh summer sun. Creosote makes a stunning backdrop for desert perennial plantings and is unsurpassed in its ability to set off a large planting of desert annuals.

One thing I like most about creosote is how much it changes through the year. In winter, with plenty of regular rainfall, creosote is a bright, dark green, luscious and full of vitality. Later in the spring, it is laden with bright yellow flowers. Soon nuts covered with white down overlay the plant. Even a light dew turns the small fruit into ornaments that glisten and sparkle in the bright spring light.

As spring progresses and the soil dries out, creosote leaves begin to turn yellow and fall. This yellowish cast is the first harbinger of summer, and eventually the plant will lose up to 75 percent of its leaves in the extended heat and drought of early summer. Then it becomes spare, a lean reminder of the long, hot summer to come.

About this time you will begin to notice creosote's marvelous branches, dark, nearly black, with a wash of ashy gray. Old growth rings form dark circles, and the plant's odd turns and erratic branching habit add to its distinctive appearance.

Pruning creosotes is particularly difficult. It is best just to remove the dead branches, which occur as a natural response to drought, because little can be done to improve on their form. More than once I have seen old, mature creosotes pruned to within inches of the ground. Plants do survive this butchery and even restore themselves vigorously with numerous new stems. For many years after such a pruning, the creosote will be green and lush, heavy with new growth, but it will lack the character and distinction of the ones left to grow naturally.

Transplanting a creosote is the same as planting any other shrub. Despite its legendary drought hardiness, a transplanted creosote requires a good deal of regular watering to get established and set a root system. Give the plant a hole much wider than it is deep and be prepared to water it daily for a week, about twice a week for a month (more if the weather is hot), and then weekly until it is well established.

Oleander

It is something of a cult in the low desert to despise **oleander** *(Nerium oleander)*. Buyers of older homes proudly announce its removal, as if this act were an initiation rite into the inner sanctum of desert gardening. Scorn drips from the lips of countless landscape students at the mere mention of the plant. But I truly like oleander; you have to admire any plant that is so daringly pretty in the face of the rigors of the long, hot, arid summer conditions of the lower desert.

Oleander is a species of the North African deserts and the Middle East, where it resides in drainages and small oases. It has been in cultivation a long time, with certain selections traced to A.D. 79. There are thought to be more than 400 cultivars, of which 175 are still in cultivation, but in Phoenix, one of the large desert cities in the world, only a fraction of that diversity is in evidence. This lack of variety in color, coupled with hideous pruning, careless placement, and overuse, has conspired to make one of the world's most drought-tolerant desert shrubs a pariah among desert gardeners. And that is a shame.

Large and full, dense and evergreen, even one oleander—and especially a hedge of oleanders—can overwhelm a small urban lot. This misuse illustrates what happens when one of the first principles of good hedges—scale—is ignored. Hedges are a part of the garden and should fit both in size and form with whatever else is happening within the garden. Gargantuan, hulking plants in areas only 10 to 12 feet wide are grotesque, swallowing everything in sight. Large properties can accept large hedges; smaller ones require something more in scale with the surroundings.

Oleanders have more uses than just as a boundary hedge. They bloom in the summer, a habit that is invaluable in the low desert. With careful early pruning, an oleander makes a good small tree or standard. Interestingly, it is successful in large containers, the container effectively creating a bonsai specimen of the plant. In or out of a pot, an oleander is easily controlled in size by the amount of water the plant receives. A long soak once a month is more than adequate to keep one in good shape and in good bloom throughout the summer in the low desert; more water simply encourages extra growth. Plants in the ground rarely need additional water in the winter. Temperatures below about 20°F damage oleanders, and temperatures below 15°F will kill them.

Any gardener who grows oleander should know that, like all members of its family, it is toxic—leaves, roots, and all. Protect your skin and eyes from exposure to the sap and from smoke if any part is burned. Because of the toxicity and toughness of the leaves, they make a poor addition to the compost pile.

Dalea

There cannot be enough good words said about the genus *Dalea*, in my opinion. Few desert gardeners are using them yet, and almost no one is acquainted with them outside the region. A number of species exist, but only bush dalea and the groundcover, trailing indigo bush *(Dalea greggii)*, are commonly available.

Bush dalea *(Dalea pulchra)* was the first dalea with which I became familiar. It is the largest of the well-known daleas, often growing 6 to 8 feet tall and nearly as wide. Its bloom, as is typical of the genus, is a tight head of purple flowers, in this case a deep magenta, accented by dense bristles, like a graceful purple broom. The foliage of bush dalea is tiny and has a distinct silvery cast. The leaves are composed of two or three pairs of leaflets, with one at the end. The shrub is evergreen and fairly dense.

Black dalea *(Dalea frutescens)* is a handsome shrub with green leaves and a full, rounded form. It grows 3 to 4 feet tall and as wide. The flowers on this dalea are a deep indigo blue held singly on the ends of the branches. The flowers are so numerous that the plant appears to change color in the fall when it blooms. The bloom begins as early as September and goes through January. The plant is semidormant in the coldest part of the winter and may produce a lot of deadwood in the lower branches. It is therefore useful to give it a hard pruning in early winter.

I have one at my front door that was paired with the clear yellow flowers of sundrops as a companion plant. The dalea overtook the sundrops, but undaunted, the sundrops has grown up and through the dalea. Now I have a yellow blooming plant in the spring and summer, when the black dalea's leaves are growing, and a stunning blue plant in the fall, often with a bit of sundrops for accent.

In the winter and earliest spring, the bloom of *Dalea versicolor* starts the cycle of year-round bloom that can be achieved with this wonderful genus of desert shrubs. The variety *sessilis* is the one most often sold. This species grows to about 4 feet tall and at least as wide. Its bloom is a tight ball of dark magenta flowers shrouded by a light film of pinkish bristles, giving the overall effect of a rosy ball on a silvery shrub. This dalea blooms a long time, from early December through at least March. I like the form of the plant, loosely rounded, with stems cascading under the weight of the bloom.

Dalea bicolor var. *argyraea* is a smaller plant, usually only 2 to 3 feet tall and as wide. It has greener leaves than the other species. The flowers, which are deep indigo, open in the fall and are very fragrant. *Dalea bicolor* var. *bicolor* is seen occasionally. It is taller, up to 5 feet, and has the intense indigo flowers so remarkable in this genus. This is a reliable fall bloomer and sometimes blooms in the spring as well.

I have been a fan of **yellow dalea** *(Dalea lutea)* for a long time and am delighted to see it finally being offered by nurseries. It is small, up to 4 feet tall and not quite that wide, and has an upright form. Creamy yellow flowers occur prolifically in the fall. Combining this species with the deep blue fall-blooming daleas would be breathtaking.

All daleas are extremely easy to grow. They do best with good drainage and watering two to three times a month in the summer for established plants and somewhat more often in the winter when they are growing and blooming. All these species grow best in full sun but will tolerate light shade.

Daleas can endure severe pruning for shape, but most have an excellent natural shape, so pruning should be minimal. All species are entirely frost hardy in the low desert.

Acacia

Guajillo *(Acacia berlandieri)* is a large lacy-leaved shrub, part of the enormous genus *Acacia*, which has so much to offer desert gardeners. Growing to about 10 feet tall and 4 to 5 feet wide, guajillo is a good backdrop to showy perennial plantings or large succulents. In spring the plant is covered with a cloud of creamy white puffball flowers, which combine with its light, ferny foliage to make this a stunning choice for a lush or tropical look.

The closely related **white-thorn** *(Acacia constricta)* and **catclaw acacia** *(Acacia greggii)* are natives in the low desert regions of Arizona that provide excellent wildlife food and shelter. Both are well armed; the white-thorn has a pair of straight thorns at each leaf node, while the catclaw has thorns that are curved. Both are good barrier and hedge plants and are undaunted by the heat, drought, and soils of the area. Both are winter deciduous, even in mild desert areas. Each flower is a small golden puffball, appearing in late spring.

Less common and much less armed are the Sonoran natives *Acacia angustissima* and *Acacia millefolia.* Both are smaller shrubs, rarely 6 feet tall and half as wide, with compound leaves. The entire leaf is delicate and graceful, looking far more luxuriant than the plant's toughness would suggest. Both species have white to cream flowers in spring. They are difficult to find but easy to use in any garden setting.

The uncommon knife-leaf acacia *(Acacia phyllodenia)* is a larger shrub, growing 6 to 8 feet tall. The leaflike phyllodes are flat but undulate in deep waves along the stem. The edge is sharp; hence, the common name. With its spare and erratically positioned stems, it is a singular specimen plant. Creamy yellow flowers appear in the early spring.

More Choices for Foliage

There are many other outstanding, though not as frequently used, evergreen desert shrubs. It is sad to me that monotony and redundancy dominate our gardening practices when there are so many desert shrubs from which to choose. I have included a good number in the pages that follow, and there are more besides.

Hopbush *(Dodonaea viscosa)* is an Arizona native species. Large, over 8 feet tall at maturity, with narrow upright, thin leaves, hopbush is a moderate water user that gives a luxurious look to a hedge or pool area.

Hopbush is particularly attractive when the winged fruit (hence, the common name) appears in late spring. This fruit varies greatly in color and size, ranging from dark burnt orange through pink-red to nearly white and from barely the size of a marble to that of a walnut. I know of only two named cultivars: 'Purpurea', which has a deep purple caste to the leaves that intensifies with cold weather, and 'Saratoga', which has uniformly dark purple leaves.

Jojoba *(Simmondsia chinensis)* has a long and varied history of uses. The nuts are edible, but too many can be upsetting to the stomach. At one time jojoba oil was promoted to replace sperm whale oil; plantation plantings are still evident along Interstate 8 in Arizona and California and south into Mexico. Jojoba oil is still used in the cosmetic trade for its emollient properties.

Jojoba is fairly large, up to 8 feet tall, and extremely dense. The leaves, which are gray-green and flattened, have the novel habit of turning inward and parallel to the sun to conserve precious moisture. Jojoba is fairly slow growing but does well under cultivation.

Arizona rosewood *(Vauquelinia californica)* is a good choice as an evergreen screen. Tall, usually 10 to 12 feet but even taller with ample water, Arizona rosewood has bright, shiny green leaves with serrated edges. The white flowers grow in a dense head. Birds eagerly devour the fruit.

Guayul or **Chisos rosewood** *(Vauquelinia corymbosa,* also known as *Vauquelinia angustifolia)* looks similar to Arizona rosewood but is just a little showier, a little more dramatic. The leaves are longer and wider, and their dark green color contrasts stunningly with the red petiole. The plant blooms prolifically, with lightly fragrant white flowers appearing in dense heads.

When I first saw the backyard of my current home, it was a sad, dull space relieved only by a large blue palo verde, a giant creosote, a wildly overgrown African sumac, and a mature **graythorn** *(Zizyphus obtusifolia)*. I was ecstatic, as I just love graythorn's gangly, tangled, silver-white stems. Graythorn is, however, a species that demands careful siting. The stems end in a thorn, and small thorns arise from the sides of the stem, making this shrub unsuitable near high-traffic areas.

Graythorn is a local native along the waterways of Arizona, but it will grow in the garden almost on natural rainfall. Watering every three to four weeks in the summer is more than adequate for a mature plant. Winter rain is important for blooming and fruiting, so during a dry winter, an occasional deep soak will help. In summer graythorn becomes a jungle gym for birds when its small black fruits are ripe.

Quail bush *(Atriplex lentiformis),* as the name implies, is a food and cover plant preferred by the charming Gambel's quail throughout the low deserts of Arizona. The plant can become large, more than 6 feet tall and as wide, and like a lot of low desert shrubs, it will grow as large or as small as its watering regime allows. Quail bush is an excellent screening shrub or informal hedge. Neither the flowers nor the fruit are showy, but birds love them. A fine example of quail bush as a hedge grows in the picnic grounds at Boyce Thompson Southwestern Arboretum.

Leaves are a soft gray and in some specimens are nearly white. There are many variations in leaf size through the species, but none of them have been selected as garden varieties.

Quail bush's close relative **four-wing saltbush** *(Atriplex canescens)* is just as large and dense, but the leaves are somewhat more heart shaped and usually much grayer. This plant has interesting winged fruit that is abundant on the plant and makes a charming addition to a dried arrangement.

For those who want to attract wildlife to the garden, there are shrubs that will especially encourage avian visitors. **Desert hackberry** *(Celtis pallida)* is a convoluted evergreen shrub that usually grows to 10 to 12 feet tall and often much wider. As branches grow low and turn down, the shrub can look like a mammoth beach ball. Desert hackberry is drought deciduous in nature—meaning, it drops its leaves when soil moisture levels get low—but with minimal supplemental watering, the plant holds its leaves throughout the year. Fruit is elusive, both because of its tiny size and because birds can strip the bush in just one day.

Desert barberry *(Berberis haematocarpa)* is one of the few good wildlife shrubs that also has showy flowers. The bright yellow flowers are prolific in the spring and are quickly followed by bright red fruit. Birds devour the fruit, often in a day, leaving nothing for seed collection if the collector's timing is not impeccable. The gray-green leaves of barberry are deeply incised, with a tiny thorn on the end, giving them the look of a gray-green holly. Barberry is a tough desert shrub and, like most Sonoran shrubs, needs occasional summer watering, but do not overdo it. I have seen barberry grow in deep shade to a good size with good leaf color and form, but it will not bloom in shade.

Another species of barberry can be found in the trade, *Berberis fremontii*. Difficult to distinguish from the desert barberry, this species comes from higher elevations and is more cold hardy.

Mexican jumping bean bush *(Sapium biloculare)* is a species with a story. Small beetles lay their eggs in the fruit, and when the fruit is warmed, the little larvae become active, wriggling and squirming in their hard-shelled cocoon. If you are holding the bean, you can feel the movement, and if you warm it sufficiently, the bean will dance around in your hand. In my childhood the beans were sold as toys, complete with fantastic explanations of why the bean could jump with no observable cause.

Little used as an ornamental, Mexican jumping bean bush is one of the most striking evergreen shrubs of the Sonoran Desert. Growing 6 to 8 feet tall, sometimes much smaller in nature, the bush has an upright form. The long, thin leaves are serrated at the edges and turn a blistering red in the winter. The flowers are unremarkable small, creamy stars, and the fruit with the little dancers is a long, hard, brown bean. It reminds me of the fruit of jojoba, to which it is not in the least related.

Little-leaf cordia (Cordia parvifolia) GARY IRISH

Copper-leaf caesalpinia *(Caesalpinia pumila)* is a large, delicate-looking shrub whose leaves are the real attraction. Rounded and small, the leaves are dark, dusky green most of the year. Then, in cooler weather, they change, first becoming rimmed with a rosy hue, then turning a rusty copper red over the entire surface. This color glows like metal in the winter light, giving the plant both its common name and its most attractive feature.

The plant can be large, over 10 feet tall and nearly as wide. Despite its size, it has a delicate symmetry and adds a lightweight touch to the garden. The flowers are the yellow typical of the genus but are small, less than 1 inch across. The fruit is a round pink pod that is held on the plant a long time, usually ripening at the same time that the leaves turn color. Together, the fruit and leaves make a charming statement that bloom is not the only way a plant can be colorful and interesting. This is a promising new shrub for the low desert area.

Most gardeners from the deep South and parts of the central United States are familiar with **redbud** *(Cercis canadensis)*, one of the first woody species to bloom in spring, bearing swirls of deep pink on bare limbs. While this species can occasionally be found here, the recent introduction of the closely related

Mexican redbud *(Cercis canadensis* var. *mexicanus,* sometimes known as *Cercis mexicanus)* should make redbud even more accessible to desert gardeners. Multistemmed, growing 8 to 10 feet tall in the best conditions, the plants are known by their dark, glossy green leaves, often charmingly enhanced by a wavy margin. As in the eastern species, the flowers are a deep pink, occasionally white, appearing before the leaves reemerge in the spring.

Mexican redbud does well in enriched soil with regular year-round irrigation. Every winter some stems die out and new shoots arise from the base. Prune out the old stems in late winter, just before the bloom starts. The plant grows steadily in the low desert, and while it does well in full sun, it thrives with a break from the western sun.

Few species of *Rhus* are native to the low Sonoran Desert, and they are not common in horticulture. Three species from high elevations, however, have been available for some time, and all do well in the lower desert.

Lemonade bush *(Rhus trilobata)* is a fine evergreen shrub from the lower Arizona chaparral vegetation zone. It grows up to 6 feet tall and just as wide and is deciduous in winter. The three-part leaves are covered with fine hairs. The flowers are unremarkable, small and white, but the fruit is a bright, deep red with a sticky surface. The fruit is delicious and has long been prized for making a soothing, cooling drink with a light, lemony flavor. This a fine shrub for a wildlife garden.

Sugarbush *(Rhus ovata)* comes and goes in the nurseries but is a lovely evergreen shrub. From the same elevations as lemonade bush, this plant grows much larger, up to 12 feet tall and 6 to 8 feet wide, and is evergreen. The leaves are large, deep green, glossy, and thick. The small, creamy white flowers, while not particularly showy, are usually abundant and are covered by an extremely attractive pink bract. The fruit is wine red and irresistible to birds. Sugarbush is sensitive to good drainage and does best with regular irrigation throughout the year.

Desert sumac *(Rhus microphylla)* is a deciduous shrub from southeastern Arizona. It has small, deep green leaves that are dense on the stems. Plants grow up to 10 feet tall and about half as wide. The flowers are typical of the genus, small, white, and not particularly showy. The sticky fruit is edible and greatly prized by birds. The leaves turn a rusty red in the fall, giving a desert illusion of fall color.

More Choices for Showy Flowers

The genus *Eremophila* represents some fine newcomers to the desert gardener's list of shrubs. The largest currently available is either a hybrid or selection of *Eremophila maculata* called 'Pink Beauty'. This plant has been around a long time, was sold locally over 20 years ago, and has made a horticultural comeback in recent years. There is good reason.

'Pink Beauty' is a large shrub, up to 8 feet tall and 6 feet wide, that can grow in almost any condition of drought, heat, or soil. It does best in full sun in unamended soil and with minimal summer watering. 'Pink Beauty' blooms in the spring from early February through March, bearing a profusion of small mauve-pink flowers. The flowers occur all along the stem at every leaf node and make a spectacular presentation. In long, cool springs it will bloom much longer.

Closely related is *Eremophila maculata*, which is a shrub 6 feet tall and 3 to 4 feet wide. The vivid deep red flowers have a cream-colored interior dotted with red, although it is hard to see this feature because the flowers turn downward. They are prolific, appearing up and down the stems in the spring. This species should be watered sparingly in the summer, particularly if the drainage is not perfect. Yellow forms are known as variety *lutea*, but not all yellow-flowered plants are the same shade of yellow. I like brighter, clearer yellows in my garden.

Eremophila decipiens is a smaller version of *Eremophila maculata*, growing 3 to 4 feet tall. Its scarlet flowers are thinner and smaller than those of *Eremophila maculata* but occur in the same fashion in the spring. My first plant of *Eremophila decipiens* was killed by accidental summer watering. This species can be hard to find.

Still uncommon but hardly destined to stay that way is *Eremophila racemosa*. I saw this species first in California and immediately brought one home. Two now live in my yard, with more to come. The flowers open a dark mauve, nearly fuchsia, but change quickly to a creamy yellow-gold and finish the color of orange sherbet. All of these colors appear on the plant at the same time because a great number of flowers are opening and closing throughout in the spring. The effect is breathtaking. I have always been a sucker for species with multiple colors on a single plant, and this is the prettiest combination I have seen.

Grown in either full sun or nearly full shade, this species blooms equally well in either exposure. Plants are less dense than other eremophilas, with numerous fine stems up to 3 feet tall. Plants grown in shade are slightly taller.

I have a good friend whose family raised cattle in South Texas. During a visit many years ago, I was struck dumb by an immense plant in her mother's backyard. It was more than 20 feet tall and coated with large, white, papery flowers that occurred in small clusters at the ends of the branches. This was my first experience with **Texas olive** *(Cordia boissieri)*, a species sadly overlooked in many of our gardens. This shrub will bloom continuously throughout the summer if provided with deep, regular irrigation. The fruit bears a resemblance to the olive but is not edible.

Texas olive performs best with regular, deep watering throughout the year. The leaves are large by desert shrub standards, rough and scratchy to the touch. They are subject to salt burn, so in areas where the water is salty, plants need long, deep soaks during the summer to alleviate the problem. While I have never seen one in Arizona reach the massive proportions of the plant in Texas, they can grow 8 to 10 feet tall.

A closely related species, **little-leaf cordia** *(Cordia parvifolia)*, is even better suited to our soils and heat. I am delighted that it is being used more and more. This species is a more moderate water user than its cousin Texas olive; deep but infrequent soaks in the summer and winter are sufficient for its sustenance.

Bright white flowers are held in small clusters at the ends of the branches. They occur intermittently throughout the summer, often in response to a good watering or a rainfall. The individual leaves are tiny (hence, the name), gray-green, and crinkled, making a smoky, ethereal backdrop for the dramatic white flowers. In mass these plants are spectacular.

Shrubby senna *(Senna wislizenii*, formerly *Cassia wislizenii)* is a much overlooked desert shrub with the admirable attribute of blooming in the hottest part of the summer. Growing to 6 feet in height and 8 feet wide, this tough desert plant will tolerate a wide range of soils. Regular summer watering, at least twice a month, will maintain the best bloom. Bright yellow flowers from June to September add great interest and color to the dark green compound leaves. The species is entirely deciduous in winter.

Both of these species, shrubby senna and little-leaf cordia, illustrate one of the great leaps of faith necessary in desert gardening. Desert shrubs often look ridiculous in a container at the nursery, offering no clue to their general shape or ultimate beauty. The stems may be sparse and grow at an odd angle in the container, but in the ground both of these species, and many others besides, will grow into a full, naturally rounded shrub.

Most desert gardeners are familiar with **red bird of paradise** *(Caesalpinia pulcherrima)* and **yellow bird of paradise** *(Caesalpinia gilliesii)*. The first plant I saw when I arrived in Phoenix was a host of red bird of paradise blooming in a roadside planting. It was astounding. I had never seen anything so brilliant.

Red bird of paradise is a small shrub with numerous stems and a generally rounded form. Plants in the low desert are rarely taller than 6 feet, but in entirely frost-free areas they can be twice that size. Red bird of paradise could set the standard for summer hardiness in the low desert. Seen throughout the hotter parts of the desert Southwest, this species is tough. It is used with ease in roadside plantings or against western walls; no place is too hot for it. It thrives in the heat, blooming best in the full sun of the low desert. Weekly watering is sufficient in the summer, although it will accept more or less.

Throughout the summer red bird of paradise produces great heads of gaudy dark orange flowers high above the lacy foliage. The petals are actually a combination of orange, reddish orange, and yellow in varying amounts and positions. Spent flowering stalks can be cut at any time to encourage more bloom. Pure yellow strains are known, but no other color selections have been identified for the species.

The complex compound leaf so common in the legume family gives the plant a feathery, light appearance. Red bird of paradise is quite frost tender, suffering leaf and tip damage at 30°F. It is best to leave the plant alone until all danger of frost is past. At that time it can be cut nearly to the ground and will regrow quickly, coming back into bloom in the summer.

Yellow bird of paradise has more of a tree form, with a strong central trunk and numerous side branches. The leaves are held sparingly on the plant and are light, compound, and feathery. The flowers are a bright yellow with 6- to 8-inch red stamens leaping out of the bloom. The flowers occur throughout the warm season, but this species will also bloom if there is a string of warm days during the winter. Just as heat tolerant as red bird of paradise, yellow bird of paradise is, however, not as cold sensitive. It is used as far north as Albuquerque in protected areas and will recover quickly from frost damage.

In less intense heat and with more summer rain, yellow bird of paradise has escaped cultivation to grow and multiply along roadsides in southeastern Arizona, but it is rarely a problem in the lower desert areas. This is a delicate, delightful plant, one for small patios and pool areas, as well as dense plantings.

Desert honeysuckle *(Anisacanthus thurberi),* a loosely arranged plant of many thin stems, grows up to 6 feet tall and bears flowers that vary from brick red to pale apricot. It is a lovely plant but difficult to use effectively because it is so subtle it is easily lost in the garden.

Notably heat and drought tolerant, this local native is a great favorite of hummingbirds. It blooms a long time and offers reliable color throughout the summer. Watering every four days in the summer keeps it in full bloom. Plants lose most or all of their leaves in the winter.

A Chihuahuan species, *Anisacanthus quadrifidus* var. *wrightii*, has become available in recent years. This, too, is a filmy sort of shrub that needs careful siting to show up its lovely summer blooming habit. The flowers are prolific little tubes of dark orange that are favored by hummingbirds.

This species benefits from a light tip pruning at intervals throughout the summer, both to increase bloom and to keep the shrub shapely. Entirely cold hardy in the low desert, it blooms best in full sun in the summer. In my opinion both of these species should be used close up, where you can appreciate the subtle, delicate range of the flowers. *Anisacanthus puberulus* is a wonder from the Chihuahuan region that has delicate mauve flowers, but you rarely see it here.

The June flowers of the **guayacan** *(Guaiacum coulteri)* are an astounding color of purple, a deep, saturated, regal shade. Guayacan is a small tree in its native region, the thorn-scrub of western Mexico, but in Arizona colder temperatures keep it a shrub.

Guayacan is best sited with overhead protection or on the highest part of the yard and needs to be covered on very cold nights. The stems are a light gray and shoot out at odd and irregular angles, giving the entire bush a confused and erratic appearance. The evergreen leaves are a clear green. Following the luscious summer bloom are brilliant red fruits held inside yellow-green bracts, which make the entire structure look like a clown's costume.

Firebush *(Hamelia patens)* comes from subtropical areas and is a fairly recent introduction from Texas into desert gardens. Plants grow rapidly to 6 feet tall with a thick set of long green leaves. In the late spring bright orange buds appear in clusters at the ends of the stems but do not open for weeks, until the weather is hot. Over the summer the narrow tubular flowers open continuously, providing ample summer color and a bounty of food for hummingbirds. Bloom lasts until the nights cool in late October. Then the foliage begins to change color, first the edges becoming tinged with orange and finally the entire leaf takes on a rusty red blush. At the same time the round dark fruit forms in clusters on the branches, matching the deepening leaves perfectly. It is hard to decide whether this plant is more pleasing for its summer bloom or its fall elegance.

Firebush loses a significant number of leaves during the winter and looks dreary and lean by early February. That is the time to prune out any dead branches and reshape as needed before the full complement of new leaves emerges in early March.

Bauhinia is a genus that includes numerous exciting ornamental species for desert gardens, most of which are very difficult to find. But **anacacho orchid tree** *(Bauhinia lunarioides,* formerly *Bauhinia congesta)* is frequently available. Forming a shrub or small tree, anacacho orchid tree grows up to 10 feet tall and is a spare, airy shrub. Its flowers are typical of the genus, an irregular form resembling an orchid, and although small, rarely over 1 inch long, are profuse on the plant. Bloom may occur anytime during warm weather but is heaviest in the late spring. Most plants that are sold have white flowers, but pink-flowering forms are known and, oddly enough, are common in natural populations. Anacacho orchid tree does best with weekly irrigation in the summer and blooms best in full sun. For a small patio or garden, this is an outstanding choice.

Tall and sometimes rangy, with long, flexible stems, **yellowbells** *(Tecoma stans)* can be a blessing on a west-facing yard. The astronomical heat that builds on a western wall or western window in the low desert can dramatically affect the comfort of the entire house. Plants that not only tolerate that much heat with a full set of leaves but also lose their leaves in the winter to allow the sun to warm the house are treasures. Yellowbells is a delightful example.

It is somewhat frost tender, dying back to the ground when temperatures drop below 25°F, and can be damaged at temperatures slightly higher. Yellowbells grows fast, however, reaching heights of 8 to 10 feet, and will recover from such damage quickly. In the low desert it is rarely killed by a freeze but will come back from the base or lower branches. It thrives on water in the summer but can tolerate great drought. Plants without ample water have fewer and paler leaves.

Of the two varieties of yellowbells, *Tecoma stans* var. *angustata* is the more cold hardy, having a native range through western Texas, southern Arizona, and northern Mexico. Its leaves are thin and finely serrated, and its bright yellow 2-inch flowers form clusters at the end of a branch.

Tecoma stans var. *stans* is more tropical in its distribution and therefore more cold sensitive. This variety has large dark green leaves that are longer and wider than those on variety *angustata*. It is a taller plant, often a small tree up to 15 feet tall, and the brilliant yellow flowers are twice as large as the ones on variety *angustata*.

There is another tecoma that merits the desert gardener's attention: the gargantuan hybrid sold as **'Orange Jubilee'**. 'Orange Jubilee' is magnificent. Its origins are fuzzy, but it is probably a hybrid of *Tecoma alata*. I bought the first one I saw at the Huntington Botanical Garden many years ago, and it has graced my front door ever since. It is now beginning to be seen in more gardens and should be more commonly used.

Tall, easily reaching 10 feet in height, it presents a veritable cascade of light orange flowers throughout the warm season. The large clusters of orange flowers begin in April and continue through the summer and fall. The thin, serrated leaves are a light green, and the flowers are held in clusters at the tips of long stems. With its height, this plant can be the perfect solution to a hot western window or a terrible view that needs to be covered in a hurry.

'Orange Jubilee' will tolerate a great deal of sun but does best with afternoon relief. Any amount of heat is fine, and it is not fussy about soil. Regular, deep irrigation throughout the summer keeps it looking its best and blooming continuously. This plant will take any amount of pruning during warm weather if it begins to outgrow its spot. Every two or three years I bring mine down to a 3-foot stump to reinvigorate it.

I have a plant that was sold to me as *Tecoma garrocha* many years ago. However, upon closer examination, Greg Starr and I are suspicious that it may be a hybrid. Regardless, both my shrub and the real *Tecoma garrocha* are lovely and should become more popular.

Tecoma garrocha has the thin light green leaves with serrated edges so common in the genus. The flowers are held in graceful, hanging clusters at the ends of the branches, so heavy they can tip the branches down. The flowers are a delicate, toasty orange lined and tipped with cream and bloom from March to November. Like most tecomas, this species will take any amount of pruning during warm weather to keep it in good shape. It is somewhat less cold tender than the others and does not lose all its leaves in the winter. It begins to look a bit worn in late winter but brightens up with new leaves during the first warm days of spring.

Along the back edge of my parents' home, a mixed hedge planted by birds separated their yard from the neighbor's horses and gardens. In among the jumble arose a spectacular **Mexican buckeye** *(Ungnadia speciosa)*, which bore brilliant pink flowers every spring. Like redbud, this species blooms before its leaves come out and then subsides into anonymity, a dark green-leaved shrub. It is winter deciduous, but in the low desert the leaves hold on longer, falling only after the weather has turned quite cold.

In its native central Texas it is a small tree, but in the low desert it rarely grows over 5 feet tall. The plant does best here in organically amended soils with steady watering throughout the year and a break from the western sun.

Indian mallow *(Abutilon palmeri)* is a Sonoran native found infrequently in drainages beneath palo verde trees. The large heart-shaped leaves are an unusual lima-bean green, sometimes nearly gray-green. They grow densely on the plant and are so covered with fine hairs that they feel like velvet. This soft plant appears much more delicate than it is.

Indian mallow blooms heavily in the spring and intermittently throughout the rest of the warm season and into fall. The flowers, which are light apricot in color, resemble tiny wide-open hibiscus, to which the plant is closely related. Spent flower clusters stay on the plant a long time and can be pruned off as soon as bloom is finished.

Indian mallow does best in a spot with protection from the western sun. It needs weekly watering in the hottest parts of the summer and irregular deep watering at other times.

The shrub known throughout the lower Sonoran desert as tomatillo is actually a collection of very similar and difficult to separate species in the genus *Lycium.* Many are also known as wolfberry. All species are modest-sized shrubs, usually from 4 to 6 feet tall at maturity, and most are entirely without leaves during warm weather. They were awarded their confusing common name (the plant has no relation to the green edible fruit tomatillo) because the fruit is small, round, and red, very much like a Lilliputian tomato. It is also very good to eat, although owing to its size, it is tedious and best left for the birds.

Of all the species, **wolfberry** *(Lycium exsertum)* is the showiest. The plant is coated with bright purple flowers in the spring that at half an inch are nearly twice the size of those in the rest of the genus. Most species bloom white, some a pale lavender, and all are prized hummingbird food when in flower and a delicacy to a host of birds when in fruit. This is an excellent wildlife choice in the garden but is best used where it will not be missed during the long leafless summer.

Blue sage *(Salvia ballotaeflora)* is a small shrub, 3 to 4 feet tall, that is winter deciduous and nearly as ornamental without its leaves as it is with them. The bare light gray branches are dainty and complex, making a fine wisp in the garden. The leaves erupt seemingly overnight in March, followed shortly by Wedgwood blue flowers that cover the plant for the rest of the summer.

Impervious to any amount of sun, blue sage grows effortlessly in slightly amended soil with regular summer watering. Cultivated like all other salvias, it is a rewarding and colorful addition to the small shrub palette. I like this shrub a lot, and sadly, though it is tough and reliable, it is not common. I have read that the dried leaves can be used to season food, but I find the pungent smell of the leaves makes that prospect unpleasant to consider.

Desert petunia *(Ruellia peninsularis)* is a 3- to 4-foot-tall shrub. Its flowers are an intense indigo blue throughout the spring and, with good irrigation, through the summer. Desert petunia is cold tender, but most damage is to the leaves, and light pruning in the early spring will bring back its good looks. With ample water it grows fast and large; with less water it remains smaller. In early summer, just when temperatures are getting warm, its seed capsules ripen and explode with mighty pops all day.

For sheer red, nothing can compare to the flowers of **Baja fairyduster** *(Calliandra californica)*. I have heard that the first specimen in the Phoenix area is the large one at the Desert Botanical Garden, on the west side of Webster Auditorium. Whether that story is true or not, it is undoubtedly one of the most handsome individuals that I have seen. Many of those currently available have become more orange than red, pale ghosts of the true species.

In a fit of organized gardening, I put a pair outside my kitchen windows many years ago in the hope that they would attract hummingbirds and provide a pleasant diversion while I was working in the kitchen. They have exceeded my wildest expectations, and that pretty much sums up the experience of everyone with this plant.

Baja fairyduster is large, up to 5 feet tall and about 4 feet wide. The species has a lot of variability both in leaf and flower color and hybridizes freely in growing yards. Plants true to the species have leaves with a dusky, dark color, and the compound leaves are densely packed on the stems. While the plant is technically evergreen, it does lose a significant number of leaves if it suffers serious drought stress or gets very cold.

The flowers are a sensational bright scarlet red, but in fact, their showy part is not petals but stamens held together in a riotous bouquet. These brilliant bristles dot the plant in red virtually year-round, pausing for a breather at the end of June and the end of winter. Hummingbirds find this plant irresistible, but I also find that verdins, wrens, and gnatcatchers like to feed on it.

Baja fairyduster adores the sun, and a western exposure is ideal for good bloom. This is the plant for the spot that is too hot for anything else or where a hot, reflective wall or pool decking could use a dash of color. It tolerates extensive drought and maintains great form and bloom with twice-a-month irrigation in the summer. Baja fairyduster is frost sensitive outside the lowest desert regions, but a covering or other overhead protection will suffice to prevent serious damage down to the mid-twenties.

Because it is always in bloom, some of us find pruning it a terrible chore. Whack away, however, because the plant recovers quickly, or if you must, wait until the short respites from blooming in early summer and late winter.

A shrub of similar endurance and lasting beauty is *Cassia purpusii*. This native of Baja will grow 5 to 6 feet tall and about half as wide. The leaves are a remote, deep gray-green, often lined with a darker shade of green or purple. Young plants and seedlings have leaves that are almost entirely purple. Throughout the winter the shrub is resplendent with bright yellow flowers, a cheery contrast to the dark foliage. This plant is impervious to heat; grow it against a western wall or in a spot too hot for anything else. Moderate water in both the winter and the summer keep it in good shape.

Feathery cassia *(Senna artemesioides,* formerly *Cassia artemesioides)* is a common Australian shrub, particularly in older desert plantings. This is a species about which I have mixed feelings. It is a pretty shrub, growing up to 6 feet tall, with numerous small, thin leaves (actually phyllodes) that range from nearly white to a light silvery green. In February it is smothered by small, rounded yellow flowers. It will take any amount of water, including only natural rainfall, and appears to have no pest or disease problems. And there is part of its problem: it has naturalized in areas where it shouldn't be.

Years ago one of my neighbors began growing it in his yard, two houses from me. Over the years he gave a couple of seedlings to nearby neighbors who admired its hardiness and its bloom. Now it is a ubiquitous pest in the entire neighborhood, growing in alleys, in waste areas that are never irrigated, coming up wherever it pleases. The same has happened in protected natural areas and parks that have plants growing adjacent to them. I recently saw this species planted along a newly revised right-of-way in Papago Park. A very ill-advised planting, it will cover the park in future years if my neighborhood (which borders the park) is any indication.

Other Australian sennas do not have such bad manners. Desert cassia *(Senna nemophila,* formerly *Cassia nemophila)* has bright, light green leaves that are so small the shrub appears to have tiny stems and no leaves at all. Bright yellow flowers appear in the winter. Another choice is silver cassia *(Senna phyllodenia,* formerly *Cassia phyllodenia).* A moderate-sized shrub, up to 6 feet, silver cassia is remarkable for its thin silver leaves (phyllodes) that move in the slightest breeze. Like most Australian members of the genus, it blooms most heavily in the winter with yellow flowers, although this species can rebloom throughout the year.

More Choices for Fragrance

There always comes a day in the spring when the unmistakable fragrance of **Texas mountain laurel** *(Sophora secundiflora)* saturates the desert garden. To some it smells like grape soda; to others it hints of wisteria; to me it is the essence of full spring. Fragrance is not common in desert shrubs, and those that provide it deserve a special place in our gardens.

Texas mountain laurel is the most regular bloomer I know of. It blooms within a week of the same day in March every year and for only a couple of weeks. I have rarely seen one vary from this timetable. Cascades of large purple flowers hang from every branch and drench the air with their sweet fragrance. After the flowers come large rounded pods that hang on the plant for over a year, holding their stone-hard, brilliant red seeds. The seeds are poisonous if eaten but are so hard that in parts of Mexico and Central America they are strung and used for jewelry.

Texas mountain laurel is a slow-growing shrub with dense, dark evergreen leaves and a rough, furrowed bark. It grows 8 to 12 feet tall. A form known as 'Silver Peso', which has white leaves, is for some reason not often seen.

Tiny tent caterpillars make their way to the tips of the branches in late spring and early summer, creating a gauzy web and feeding on the new growth. On large plants they are a simple matter to prune out or kill by hand as soon as they are seen, but on smaller plants too much pruning can set the plant back, so just remove the caterpillars by hand.

Beebush *(Aloysia wrightii)* is a tall shrub, up to 8 feet high and half again as wide, that provides a powerful sweet smell to summer gardens. The shrub has branches that rise and fall back to the ground, a feature that causes it to take up a great deal of room when left to its own devices. It can be rigorously pruned to a more manageable size or even into a standard.

Aloysia is a genus with a complicated taxonomic history. Some members are assigned to the genus *Lippia*, while others are assigned to *Aloysia*, and there is much moving back and forth by botanists. All are fragrant, and many are edible. *Lippia graveolens* grows well here, and its leaves are dried and sold as Mexican oregano. *Aloysia wrightii* is a more common species and a local Sonoran native. It is virtually indistinguishable from the eastern *Aloysia lycioides*.

Beebush provides excellent bee and insect food, as well as good cover for quail and other ground-dwelling birds. The flowers are tiny and white, occurring in dense clusters at the ends of the stems. The smell is evocative, a heady mixture of vanilla and jasmine that floats like gossamer on humid evenings. The species is cold deciduous, losing most but not all of its leaves in the coldest part of the winter. Early spring is a good time to give the plant a heavy pruning to maintain good shape and get rid of the many small dead branches of winter.

Less common in gardens but a wonderfully scented shrub is **bitter condalia** *(Condalia globosa)*. The common name refers to the fruit, which has a bitter taste to humans but is relished by birds. This is a large shrub, often a tree, growing 12 feet tall or more. The branches end in tiny thorns, and with its complicated branching pattern, bitter condalia makes a daunting hedge or barrier planting. It is an extremely rugged shrub; older established plants can live entirely on their own in the garden.

The minuscule flowers open in late winter but are difficult to see. It never ceases to amaze me that such a lilliputian flower produces such a powerful smell; one large shrub's scent will fill an entire garden. The smell is both sweet and acrid, unmistakable once known. The dark, black, round fruits that follow are candy to the birds.

Desert lavender *(Hyptis emoryi)* is a much overlooked common Sonoran native. This lovely shrub has tiny gray-green leaves held close to the stem and an overall upright form. Tiny lavender flowers appear in the spring and sometimes in the fall. The foliage releases its scent with a tiny pinch. This species likes extremely good drainage, the rockier the better, and rarely requires anything more than intermittent watering once it is established. Being overwatered and growing on too rich soil can cause the plant to become overgrown and floppy and lose its characteristic smell.

Red bird of paradise (Caesalpinia pulcherrima) *MARY IRISH*

5 *Perennials*

$\mathcal{M}$oder gardeners take perennial gardening for granted, but this wasn't always so. Prior to the eighteenth century, French, Italian, and Spanish gardens defined garden style in Europe and represented the premier gardens of their time. These gardens were inspired by the brilliant Moorish designs of the even older gardens of North Africa. Moorish gardens were rich in detail, and plantings were exact and usually symmetrical. Because texture was used to establish contrast and interest, foliage was the primary feature of the plants, and both the plants and the gardens were developed into rigorously regular forms, often by meticulous pruning. Gardens were often hidden or enclosed, havens and respites from the noise and business of everyday life. Gardeners in the Southwest are heirs to this heritage, which is typified by courtyards and patios, small water features and fountains, tile work, and porches covered with colorful vines.

As the wealth of eighteenth-century England increased and plant explorers returned from the Americas and Asia with many new species, gardens changed. The English gardener became a trendsetter in garden fashion, creating elaborate, extravagant beds of annuals that featured the detailed use of color. Because this practice required that plants be rotated three or four times a year, it required exorbitant expenditures of money and became a means of showing off the wealth of the empire.

Eventually such excess produced a backlash, which began with the gardens and writings of William Robinson and Gertrude Jekyll in the late nineteenth century. These garden designers and writers advocated a shift in gardening style toward more relaxed, naturalistic plantings as a counterpoint to the stiff gaudiness of late Victorian gardens.

Using woodlands and natural areas, including old cottage gardens, as their models, English gardeners began to favor perennials to express this style. Perennials are easier and more permanent, less labor intensive and cheaper, which appealed to the burgeoning middle class. This type of garden was for everyone, not just the wealthy aristocracy. It did not require great estates or armies of gardeners to be effective.

Gardens both here and in Europe were profoundly influenced by this trend. The cottage garden with lots of plants in lots of colors or the more formal lawn outlined by graceful perennial beds became the standard of gardening on both sides of the Atlantic throughout the twentieth century.

In the latter part of the twentieth century, American gardeners also developed an increasing interest in native plants, resulting in gardens with strong regional presence. Less lawn, more shrubs and perennials, and greater numbers of natives and wildflowers are themes that define the outline of American gardens today.

Perennials in the Garden...

These themes are particularly attractive to desert gardeners because of the conditions and requirements particular to our climate and soils. Desert perennials are excellent garden plants, rugged, long lasting, and extremely colorful. Desert gardens also enjoy a unique component of perennial plantings—succulents in fascinating variety. With rare exception, such succulents as aloe, agave, cactus, and mesemb are perennial and can be outstanding additions to a good perennial garden. The winter bloom of aloes and mesembs makes them particularly useful to gardeners for year-round interest, and the sharp, crisp forms of agaves and smaller yuccas help emphasize the desert nature of a garden and relieve the endless burden of wide green leaves.

We use perennials in various ways: to provide accents in a small planting, to complement trees and large shrubs, to provide color through long seasons, and to attract the hordes of butterflies, birds, and other wildlife that depend on them for food and shelter.

Perennial Borders

The most common expression of gardening with perennials is the so-called perennial border. The name comes from English gardening, in which a border of perennials evolved at the edge of the lawn. Perennial borders can be astoundingly sophisticated. Outstanding perennial borders glide gently through the seasons as first one, then another group of plants blooms brilliantly, each fading into the background as it is replaced. As in a corps de ballet, the plants emerge, entice, and retreat. Nothing remains on stage too long; every round of bloom subtly suggests the next, like a glorious rainbow with no end and no beginning. Such perennial plantings are meant to be viewed as you walk by and through them, as well as from one or two well-placed resting locations. They are planted accordingly.

This challenging but extremely pleasant design scheme is rarely used in the desert, which I think is a shame. Instead of bordering a lawn, a perennial border in the desert could anchor a long path or driveway or surround a paved area. Successful perennial borders demand a solid knowledge of the plants, making them the ultimate plantsman's garden. They also demand some discipline in selection and maintenance: not all combinations are successful, and plants must be removed or replaced no matter how much you love them or how hard they were to grow.

I urge anyone with an interest in manipulating color and form in the garden to give the perennial border a try. It is harder than it looks, but is most rewarding. The dictates of perennial garden design are widely discussed in gardening books, but one thing is certain: setting the bones of such a garden is important. Plopping a large number of species together, no matter how individually interesting, does not make a perennial border. While the results may be pleasant, such a random approach rarely achieves the year-round color and delicate complements and balances of a true perennial border.

Mixed Plantings

Mixing perennials and succulents is one of the true delights of the desert garden. Watering the bed, however, requires extra attention. Drip irrigation makes this somewhat easier because emitters can be set on the perennials and not on the succulents, so that the succulents are not saturated but receive the benefit of adjacent water. If watering by hose, direct most of the water on the non-succulent perennials.

Succulents with strong seasonal dormancy, like boojums, some haworthias, bulbines, sansevierias, and selected cacti, are not suitable for mixed plantings. Species that strongly resist summer (or winter) watering, such as *Salvia canariensis*, *Medicago arborea*, and many woody Mediterranean salvias, do not mix well with plantings that receive water year-round.

Rock Gardens

In our yard my husband uses a combination of lavender cotton, turpentine bush, damianita, Angelita daisy, buckwheat, white bush morning glory, and rosemary to achieve a desert rock garden look. Rock gardens in more temperate climates are usually composed of high-elevation species that grow low and mounding. But the rock garden look has developed beyond one group and is now thought of as a collection of regularly shaped plants put together for color and textural interest, often on a slope or hillside.

I think desert species lend themselves to this style. The desert rock garden is a work in progress, and progress is slow, the worst problem being a tendency to set plants too close together, leaving little room for them to develop without interference and contortion by the neighbors. So far we are happy with the results in our rock garden. I like the way the planting follows the steps down to the vegetable garden.

Color Schemes

If there were no color, I wonder if we would garden at all. When you see exuberant spring bloom or the perfect pairing of blues and whites or are stopped in awe by a hillside of brittlebush and globemallow, you cannot help but feel that color is really the purpose of gardening after all. Most of the time I do not really believe that is the case, but gardening might not be so much fun without those riveting color displays.

Some colors have a natural affinity for each other; blue, gray, and white combined in any way make one another look better. Red can be more difficult to combine, but look closely at the red to see if there is more blue in it (making it closer to purple) or more white (making it closer to pink). Try my favorite method for the imagination-deprived (I am a charter member): if a color combination looks good, leave it; if it doesn't, move the offending plant and substitute another color. You have only yourself to please.

Color theme gardens can be deeply satisfying in the right location. Yellow and gray or gray alone would be interesting in the low desert, and there are so many desert plants to choose for that combination. The cooling tones of blue-white-gray can help tone down a hot spot or lighten a dark one. An all-white garden has marvelous possibilities in the desert, owing to the large number of white-colored night bloomers, lots of nice evenings to enjoy them, and their intoxicating array of fragrance.

Planting, Watering, and Pruning...

When I gardened on the Gulf Coast, I was accustomed to standing back and watching newly planted perennials fill in the garden within the same year. In Arizona you need more patience; most perennials take up to three years to be fully established and looking their best.

Fall planting is ideal for almost all desert perennials, although spring planting will work if you give careful attention to watering. Summer dormant plants or those from winter rainy areas are most responsive to fall planting. Plants such as rosemary, white sage, and *Salvia clevelandii* can be tricky to get to set properly in the spring.

Like trees, perennials are best planted in a hole about the depth of the container and four to five times wider. Even the most rugged natives enjoy a little enrichment added to the soil in order to look their best in a perennial planting, so mix compost or composted mulch into the backfill when planting. Frequent fertilization is unnecessary and can even be harmful to desert perennials. I spread an organic mix of compost and mulch twice a year on my garden for fertilization and soil enhancement. If you use inorganic fertilizers, an application just before growth gets underway (usually early fall) and one in late winter are sufficient.

Watering perennials takes practice because they do not all have the same needs. I include specific suggestions for individual plants below, but in general, established herbaceous perennials need to be watered every three to four days when it is hot and dry (generally May and June in our area) and every four to five days when it is over 95°F or the humidity is higher (generally July to September). Cool-season watering depends on the temperature and how much rainfall there is. Most established desert perennials respond admirably to watering two or three times a month from November to February. Species that are natives of the Sonoran Desert are often winter growing; generous winter watering schedules will help them bloom vigorously in the spring.

Almost all herbaceous perennials look healthier and fuller if they are pruned from time to time. The best time is directly after flowering, but if flowering is a long-term affair, prune the plant just before the principal growing season. With rare exceptions, do not prune during the hottest part of summer or the coldest part of winter. Pruning is best done when plants are growing quickly or soon will be. Unlike a woody shrub or a tree, perennials can be sheared off nearly to the ground. Done at the proper time of the year, this sort of pruning greatly invigorates a perennial and can result in better bloom.

Perennial Choices...

Red-Flowered Perennials

Thinking of red brings the genus *Salvia* to mind, particularly **scarlet sage** *(Salvia coccinea)*. This species grows from North Carolina through eastern Texas and across southern Texas and into Mexico. Perhaps originally native to Mexico, scarlet sage has been in cultivation since the end of the eighteenth century. Annual in cooler climates, it is perennial in the low desert. I have known this species for a long time from my aunt's garden in Texas; it is popular in the hot, humid gardens of the South.

The flowers are nonsymmetrical, with the distinctive hood and lower lip typical of the genus, and are deep scarlet red. They are held upright on 6- to 9-inch stalks above the 2- to 3-foot-tall plants. Numerous color variants exist within the species—'Lactea', with bright white flowers on deep green foliage; a pink known as 'Brenthurst'; and assorted bicolors, salmons, and pinks—all of which are lovely but none of which I have found as confident in the garden as the familiar old red. 'Lactea' deserves more attention in the low desert, as it does well in light shade. 'Lady in Red' blooms an extremely dense shade of red.

Scarlet sage is exceedingly heat tolerant but needs supplemental summer water in order to thrive in the low desert. Watering every three to four days in summer is sufficient. In good garden conditions it becomes a benign weed and will reseed, spreading throughout the yard, although never far from water. Rangy and gangly on its own, this species needs regular vigorous pruning. It works best in a mass or amid a lot of other plants. The form and bloom improve with severe pruning after every flowering, which lasts from March to November, and it responds particularly well to a severe pruning in late February.

Autumn sage *(Salvia greggii)* is a terrible misnomer for a species that blooms almost throughout the year. This is a good plant for desert gardens, but its culture is frequently misunderstood and it suffers from overuse and bad planting. Autumn sage does best in enriched soils with regular watering in summer. It grows well in light shade or with an eastern exposure. If grown in full sun, it needs water every two to three days in the summer, as well as a heavy mulch or crowded conditions to keep the roots cool. Given this culture, it grows effortlessly and sends up tall spikes of wide-lipped red flowers from March through November. Autumn sage should be pruned after each flowering and cut back regularly through the summer until early October.

The plants are 3 feet tall with the bloom. The color of autumn sage is generally a deep rosy red, a red with quite a bit of blue, but there are countless other shades. Some of these are named: 'San Antonio', a bicolor with cream and apricot that does poorly here; 'Furman's Red', which is really more of a magenta and does well; 'Desert Red', which is a deep velvet red and is most likely the same as a number of other red cultivars; 'Alba', which is white; 'Big Pink', aptly described by its name; 'Cherry Red', a popular cultivar in the South; 'Purple Haze', which has small, intensely violet flowers; and 'Purple Pastel', a good repeat bloomer in the fall. There is a hybrid group of this species and *Salvia microphylla*, named *Salvia* x *jamensis*, and some of the so-called *Salvia greggii* cultivars are actually part of this group. I found a wonderful cultivar in Texas years ago, which I call 'Texas Red', which is undoubtedly part of this group. It has exceptionally large flowers of a deep, rich red and large rounded leaves.

Cherry sage *(Salvia microphylla)* is a confusing species for gardeners. It can be extremely difficult to distinguish from autumn sage, as both are highly variable in both leaf and flower forms and an unknowable number of hybrids abounds. Cherry sage has a wide natural distribution from southeastern Arizona into eastern Mexico. It is generally a fragrant plant; crushing the leaves releases a pungent, pleasant aroma. This species is generally more drought, sun, and heat tolerant than autumn sage. It is usually red, but there are also other color forms. 'Rosita' is a bright pink, and 'San Carlos Festival' is a full and leafy plant with magenta-pink flowers. There are European cultivars of this plant as well, particularly 'Oxford', a dark magenta-crimson; 'Cerro Potosi', with large magenta flowers; and 'Pink Blush', which is pink. Cherry sage takes the same culture as scarlet sage and, like all the red sages, is exceptionally attractive to hummingbirds.

For situations with even more shade and water, **red betony** *(Stachys coccinea)* is a wonderful choice. The plant will reseed if it is happy, even into nearby potted plants. For me it is short-lived and easily yellows with overwatering, but its aggressive reseeding is a boost to its popularity. In places with slightly more benign climates, like Tucson, Superior, or Globe, the plant grows 3 to 4 feet tall during the summer.

Winter is a good time for red bloom in the desert garden. **Chuparosa** *(Justicia californica)* is resplendent through most of the winter, producing delicate tubular red flowers on thin stems. Old plants can have hundreds of stems and grow to 6 feet tall or more, producing a saturation of red that leaves hummingbirds in a swoon of nectar. The flowers are tasty, resembling the flavor of cucumber, and make a good addition to salads. Easy to grow in gravelly, well-drained sites, this species is often cantankerous and slow to start in other locations. Your patience will be rewarded, and you can be mollified by the fact that chuparosa will bloom when small. This plant makes a distinctive vignette when planted at the base of an ocotillo, desert tree, or other woody desert shrub. While it can grow in extreme full sun, in many gardens it is equally happy in a partially shaded location, but drainage should be excellent. Like many desert plants, chuparosa works best if it is watered infrequently but deeply.

Yellow-flowered forms can be found from time to time. A bicolor with yellow tube and pale orange lips, called 'Tecate Gold', and a bright yellow-flowered form known as 'Dick Tilford' are lovely, though infrequently available.

A near relative, **red justicia** *(Justicia candicans,* formerly *Justicia ovata)* is tolerant of a wide range of soils, sunlight, and watering conditions. This is one of the most effortless species I can think of for desert gardens, particularly when you consider its rewards. Red justicia blooms almost continuously but is most luxuriant in the winter. Bloom begins (if it ever stopped) before Christmas and continues unabated until late spring, becoming more sparse and intermittent through the hot summer.

This species responds to light pruning anytime, but a good shaping can be done during summer or in early fall. It generally has a growth spurt in late spring or early summer, when bloom is reduced, and again at the end of the monsoon, from mid-September to October. I have seen this plant used to good advantage in large containers, as a filler for a narrow spot, and as a point of color in a small courtyard.

Both chuparosa and red justicia have a reputation for being cold sensitive, with damage occurring below 25°F. Native populations endure much more cold than that in western Arizona, and I have never seen a red justicia more than nipped by a cold snap. Should damage occur, however, a good pruning when the weather warms, combined with the plant's quick growth habit, will remedy any damage rapidly.

Red penstemon *(Penstemon eatonii)* is a brilliant scarlet-blooming plant that grows naturally out of rock faces. This offers the shrewd gardener a clue about its drainage requirements. Red penstemon requires rocky-sharp drainage and tolerates full sun or partial shade. I like to see it planted where its droopy, flopping form works best, such as backing up to a wall or hanging over a container. In the ground by itself, it tends to look overwrought. A lot of good desert canyon species like the combination of cool roots and a hot head, the perfect cultural conditions for this perennial penstemon. It blooms once, in March in the lowest desert, later at higher elevations. The flowers are a deep, clear red on a 2-foot-tall inflorescence that is usually not straight. It needs to be moderately watered in the summer; overwatering will cause the plant to rot.

Most desert penstemons are dormant in the summer, but the sturdy **rock penstemon** *(Penstemon baccharifolius)* is a lovely exception. Originally I grew it to fill in for spring-flowering plants in a hummingbird planting, and it is now a great favorite. Hummingbirds love this penstemon. Growing well throughout the cool season, the plant reaches 2 feet in height and is about as wide. Bloom does not begin until hot weather and will continue throughout the summer with watering every three to five days. As with salvias, it is a good practice to trim back old blooming stalks for a continued bloom, and in fact this plant blends well with salvias. I trim mine back severely in the late winter to invigorate it.

Occasionally rock penstemon will look tired, sagging in the middle, leaves turning brown. Usually this is a sign of overwatering, so just cut back the ragged growth and reduce the frequency of watering and soon the plant will recover. Rock penstemon can take a great deal of sun and demands little care except supplemental irrigation in the summer.

The uncommon **bush snapdragon** *(Galvezia juncea)* is a Baja native to which I have been drawn, but it appears to be short-lived in my garden, perhaps because of the heat of Phoenix summers. Plants in Tucson seem to fare much better.

Bush snapdragon grows to be 3 to 4 feet tall, with reedlike stems. The red tubular flowers bloom from spring through summer, quit when it is hot, then resume in the fall. This species is highly attractive to hummingbirds. Overwatering makes it floppy, as does too much shade.

A good choice for the shade is **bat flower** *(Cuphea llavea)*. It does not bloom as long as its close relative cigar plant *(Cuphea ignea)*, but it is much more curious. Its small, brilliant scarlet petals are flattened, revealing a deep purple interior that looks remarkably like the face of a bat. Bat flower benefits from an enriched soil and twice-a-week irrigation in the low desert. In higher elevations this species can be grown in increasing amounts of sun, even full sun if kept well watered.

Pink-Flowered Perennials

Pink, the fairer cousin of red, is a color of extremes, from pale pastels to hot, vibrant hues. At the delicate end is the nearly translucent pink of **Mexican primrose** *(Oenothera speciosa,* formerly *Oenothera berlandieri)*. In certain situations this species is a pernicious and persistent groundcover; in others it is more genteel. It enjoys full sun, good drainage, and can take as little or as much water as suits the gardener. Spreading by rooting stems, as well as by seed, it will spread quickly in a congenial spot. Cutting it back severely in the summer or fall helps keep it under control.

Mexican primrose blooms in the spring at the height of the desert spring bloom. Flea beetles feed on the leaves in late spring, leaving round cutouts, but the damage is rarely more than a cosmetic problem.

Pink fairyduster *(Calliandra eriophylla)* is native to the upper Sonoran Desert. A 2- to 3-foot-tall plant, it bears light pink flowers in February and March. The color ranges from a deep, dark cerise to white. The species is extremely drought tolerant: well-established individuals need no supplemental irrigation but will be deciduous in the summer without it. With irrigation they will bloom two or three times during the long desert spring.

Parry's penstemon *(Penstemon parryi)* is unrivaled for its dependable spring bloom and ability to tolerate demanding desert conditions. In fact, treating a plant too well will certainly result in its death. A small plant, less than 12 inches tall, this penstemon has somewhat linear leaves and a 3- to 4-foot blooming stalk in the spring. The bright pink flowers are tubular with flared tips; they make excellent cut flowers and are irresistible to hummingbirds.

Seeds will germinate readily after direct seeding in October, with new plants often blooming the following spring. The plant grows throughout the spring, rests in the hottest part of the summer, begins a terrific growth spurt the following winter, and has a magnificent bloom in the second spring. Small plants set out in the fall will have already grown nearly a year by the following spring and can be spectacular.

While Parry's penstemon responds to lightly amended soil, it also thrives in rocky, dry soil. It is important not to overwater the plants in the summer, as brief, occasional watering is all that is needed. Rabbits like the stalks, and after one of these miserable moochers took off some of the best of my 4-foot stalks one spring, I was delighted to find that the plant grew another set—much thinner and shorter but lovely nonetheless.

This species reseeds prolifically, especially if the soil has rocks or a rocky groundcover. Within three years what begins as a small group of Parry's penstemon becomes a nursery of penstemons, and you will find yourself moving and pulling them to rearrange the astounding numbers of plants. The seed can be saved for many years if it is well dried and then stored in the refrigerator in a moisture-proof container.

Canyon penstemon *(Penstemon pseudospectabilis)* is one of my great favorites, though not as common in gardens as Parry's penstemon. Rising to 3 feet on many stems, it has serrated leaves with the curious habit of surrounding the stalk, thereby distinguishing canyon penstemon from Palmer's penstemon, which also has serrated leaves. The flower, a fuchsia pink, is smaller and less open than Parry's or Palmer's. Canyon penstemon likes a richer soil and infrequent irrigation in the summer. While it is not as reliable a reseeder as Parry's penstemon, a few small plants will show up here and there.

Penstemon superbus is a large penstemon with hefty, thick leaves on plants that are 8 to 12 inches tall. In the spring reddish stalks rise 6 to 8 feet, bearing coral flowers. This is a commanding garden plant best used in the back of a mixed planting. It requires culture similar to all the desert penstemons.

Palmer's penstemon *(Penstemon palmeri)* is astonishing. The blooming stalk rises 6 feet high, and the large flowers look like mauve-pink bells on a grand stem. Native over a large region in the West, this penstemon is cold hardy to the high teens. Outstanding native populations grow in the mountains between Prescott and Jerome, as well as on the sere hillsides west of Wickenberg.

When we first moved into our present house, our neighbors were Howard and Marie Gentry, he a botanist of great repute for his work on agaves. In their backyard they had an amazing stand of Palmer's penstemon that I envied greatly because mine rarely made it through the summer. He and I sealed what interest we had in each other over our admiration for this native penstemon species. He had grown it for some time as a cut flower in California, and I am still puzzled why it is not more common in southern Arizona. When I wanted to know the secret behind his enormous stand of Palmer's penstemon, he said it might be that they were growing in rocky soil. But I noticed that we both had rocky soil. I think the difference between his glorious specimens and mine was that his faced north, thereby relieving them of great stress in the summer, while mine struggled on the southern side of the house, and his received minimal summer water, while mine got quite a lot. Subsequent years of trying to grow Palmer's penstemon have borne these cultural tips out.

Some of the most reliable and lovely species for the desert gardener's repertoire have come from Texas. *Pavonia lasiopetala* stands as a great addition to the list. A low, compact shrub 3 feet tall, it blooms a deep pink from late spring through summer. The flowers are about 1 inch across and open wide. Hard pruning early in the spring and again after the first flush of bloom will keep the plant compact. Pavonia can become chlorotic in late summer, often the result of too much water in the midst of hot weather. Cut back on the watering, and it will be fine once the weather cools down. This charming plant deserves more attention.

A few years ago in Palm Springs, I saw an irresistible salvia named *Salvia canariensis*. I brought a couple of plants back to Phoenix, but they failed to survive the summer in pots. I tried again and the second group is doing well, although like many salvias, this species has proved to be short-lived.

The plant can become large, over 4 feet tall, when watered a lot but can be kept to 2 to 3 feet if grown a little leaner. It thrives in unamended, well-drained rocky soil but does appreciate a break from the full afternoon sun. The leaves are large and gray-green, and the stems are covered with a soft, white blush. The bloom is extremely showy, a large spike of dark rose-red flowers covered by a mauve bract. This species is difficult to find but is bound to become more common, owing to its startling beauty.

Orange-Flowered Perennials

As yellow begins to overtake red on the spectrum, orange and its countless subtle variations emerge. The color of summer, orange is such a hot, bright hue that it easily dominates; I find that some oranges are nearly impossible to use effectively. Used with restraint and recognition of its eye-catching properties, however, orange can enliven and enrich a summer garden.

I do not particularly care for the color of **hummingbird bush** (*Justicia spicigera*), partly because of its pale yellow-green leaves. Used effusively, badly, and sadly, hummingbird bush is now a cliché in the Phoenix area. That is a shame, because it is a reliable and long-blooming plant. Too often planted in full sun in hot locations, it fades in both foliage and flowers. Planted in too much shade, it blooms, but the stems and leaves elongate in an unhealthy etiolated state. It produces better-looking leaves and flowers in light shade, such as under high mesquites or palo verdes. Hummingbird bush will bloom almost year-round and is effective in mass plantings. Hummingbirds adore it. Twice-a-year applications of manure or compost spread around the roots will help keep it vigorous. It does not require annual pruning, but cutting it back severely every few years keeps it in good form.

For a big splash and nearly continuous bloom, I like **firewheel** *(Gaillardia aristata),* a perennial member of this typically annual genus. I first planted this species from seed and was delighted when it not only came up but bloomed throughout that same summer. Plants fade in late fall and nearly disappear in winter, with only a small basal set of leaves remaining. But in the spring those leaves begin to grow, and new seedlings emerge. Firewheel will fill the entire garden if you are not vigilant, but in the early spring small plants can be moved with impunity.

Firewheel blooms from March through November and sometimes even in winter. It is a studious flower, deep and brooding, not bright and lively like sunflowers, and I could never be without it. The flower is a wheel of petals around a dark brown center and comes in various combinations of brown, red-brown, and yellow on the petals.

Every fall **California fuchsia** *(Zauschneria californica)* emerges from its green sleep and cloaks itself in a swath of orange. Graceful falls of nodding red-orange flowers can begin as early as September but are more common later in the fall. One year my plant began blooming in May and continued until November, a feat it has yet to repeat.

California fuchsia needs room, spreading quickly from runners, which makes it a great choice for closing a corner or for a mass planting. From a 1-gallon plant, regardless of how puny, within two years a vigorous 2-foot-tall plant full of bloom will emerge. The species is extremely fragile during transplanting or moving and will fall apart, causing great consternation in the gardener. Almost as compensation, however, it is extraordinarily root hardy. The smallest section of intact root, no matter how much or how little stem and leaf is attached, will take root and grow, allowing recovery from even the most devastating dismemberment. The plant responds well to a hard pruning in early winter, late January, or February to remove old stems and allow the growth of new ones. It can be pruned anytime throughout the spring to increase its fullness, but pruning in the summer will reduce bloom.

Once on a visit to Houston I saw a charming plant coming up out of the sidewalk. Thinking it pretty and noticing it had seed, I brought it home. To my delight, it turned out to be **bloodflower** *(Asclepias curassavica)*, one of the massive tribe of milkweeds, and it is completely at home in my garden.

The flower of bloodflower is made up of vivid orange petals that lie like a skirt around the dark golden vases of the corona, a structure distinctive to this family. It is irresistible to most butterflies, particularly monarchs. The plants grow 2 feet tall and have thin leaves. They are somewhat frost tender and look pitiful by the end of winter. Cut the foliage back to the ground anytime in the winter, and the plant will emerge from the base in March. Grown in either full sun or partial shade, bloodflower is appealing for its long summer bloom.

This milkweed, like all milkweeds in my experience, floats its characteristic plumed seed all over the garden to germinate in the most unlikely places. I am prone to leaving most of the seedlings because butterflies like them and they bloom even in hot weather, but we each must decide the extent of weediness we can tolerate in the garden. On the plus side, I have never found this species growing in the alley, along the roadside, or anywhere outside the gentle soils and extra water of a garden.

While almost anything grows well in light shade here in the low desert, deep shade is a challenge to any gardener anywhere. One of the finest deep-shade bloomers I have found for the low desert is **cigar plant** *(Cuphea ignea)*. Grown throughout the world as a perennial in warm areas and an annual in cold climates, this is a beautiful summer bloomer full of little tubular orange flowers tipped with yellow, reminiscent of a cigar. Some forms have dark purple at the tip and are also quite attractive.

Growing up to 4 feet tall, cuphea attracts hummingbirds. The plant looks dreary in late winter, when most of the leaves are gone and those that remain are yellow and pitiful. This is a temporary state, however, one common to subtropical species in late winter, and it will pass. Seemingly overnight, the plant takes heart, greens up, and almost immediately begins to bloom.

Yellow-Flowered Perennials

Yellow may be the color of summer or fall in some areas but in the desert it signals spring. This is when two great native perennials, desert marigold and brittlebush, come into their full glory.

Desert marigold *(Baileya multiradiata)* is common along disturbed roadsides in the desert at low elevations and will do well in most gardens if you can get it going. The plants are small and have deeply incised gray, fuzzy leaves that form a low, loose rosette. Long, thin flower stalks emerge in early spring, each topped by a single flower, which is open, multipetaled, and bright yellow. In older plants there can be dozens of flowering stalks, and in favorable conditions the plants will bloom year-round.

Desert marigold is cranky about growing from seed. Some years it comes up easily; in other years it is nearly impossible, showing up at the most unlikely times in the most unlikely places, long after you've forgotten that you planted it. Transplants put out in the fall are extremely successful at any size and remain vigorous for years. If you are lucky enough to have small seedlings come up in your garden, they can be easily and successfully moved from November to January.

Like many desert perennials, desert marigolds enjoy a fairly dry summer and a good deal of sun. Nice garden soil will kill them, as will too much water in the summer. I do not find many seedlings in my yard, but the ones I do find are in absurd locations, such as the pavementlike area under the drip line of the roof. I have moved every one of them, thus far successfully. Someday I hope to have enough desert marigolds in my desert garden to be able to quit moving them.

Brittlebush *(Encelia farinosa)* coats the hillsides of the small buttes and hills of southern Arizona. It is one of those plants that you do not realize is so common until it blooms, igniting entire hillsides with its bright yellow flowers. It grows about 3 feet tall and with irrigation can get much larger, but not necessarily prettier. The whitish cast to the gray-green leaves comes from hairs that are responsive to water—the less water, the whiter they are. Overhead watering or too much watering will diminish the whiteness.

Brittlebush sends up long-stalked yellow flowers as early as October but more usually in January or February. Overgrown plants can be cut back in the late spring or early fall to reinvigorate their shape. This species does best with infrequent watering to remain healthy and vigorous through the summer. I have dozens that grow entirely on their own, and I enjoy their curled white leaves in the summer; the plant looks like a fossil in foggy amber. Others with infrequent summer watering do not get so crispy but keep their shape and white leaf color.

Shrubby alfalfa *(Medicago arborea)* is a marvelous addition to a winter garden. Entirely dormant in the summer, when only its stark, gray stems remain, shrubby alfalfa undergoes a metamorphosis in the fall as dark green leaves emerge and fill out the plant. Dense and green, shrubby alfalfa becomes an accent for any winter color. Bloom begins in early January and is prolific through late March or April. The bright yellow flowers stay on the plant through the entire winter. By April they have faded and the leaves begin to turn a pale golden yellow, sometimes remaining for a long time on the plant.

Shrubby alfalfa thrives in full sun with superb drainage and minimal summer water. The plants have a naturally compact form and grow to 4 feet tall.

One of the last flowers to come into bloom is **Mt. Lemmon marigold** *(Tagetes lemmonii)* and its near relative Mexican mint marigold *(Tagetes lucida)*. Mt. Lemmon marigold is loose and light, with delicate, finely dissected leaves and golden yellow flowers that bloom profusely. It has a pungent, sharp scent that is released by rubbing the foliage or just brushing against the plant as you pass by. This species blooms best in the lowest desert with light shade, but in Tucson and other higher locations it does well in full sun. Culture is similar to that for salvias—a somewhat enriched soil that cools the roots. Cut it back in the late fall after it blooms to keep the shape of the plant.

Mexican mint marigold, also called Mexican tarragon, has much darker green leaves that are long and thin. The leaves are profuse, giving the plant a dense, full appearance. They give off a pungent smell, like that of tarragon or anise, and in fact make a good culinary substitute for tarragon, which is difficult to grow in the low desert. The flowers are a deep yellow with hints of gold. The plants grow 3 feet tall and about 2 to 3 feet wide and are deciduous in the winter. A hard pruning just before they leaf out will invigorate them.

Years ago, when I had just become acquainted with Mexican mint marigold, I met a woman at the Desert Botanical Garden plant sale who was ecstatic to see the species. Her mother had grown it and made a tea from the leaves, and the plant brought back a host of memories to her. The tea she recommended is delicious, soothing, and smooth, a simple infusion of the leaves with hot water and honey.

Easily confused with each other, **turpentine bush** *(Ericameria laricifolia)* and **damianita** *(Chrysactinia mexicana)* are low, tight, small-leaved, woody-stemmed perennials. Both are wonderful bright green plants with tiny compressed leaves set so closely together the entire plant looks like a bouquet. Both have brilliant yellow flowers. One of the easiest ways to distinguish them is by the smell of the leaf. Turpentine bush is pungent, strong, and well named: it smells exactly like turpentine. Damianita smells sharp and earthy, without the chemical overtone.

Damianita will bloom most prolifically in the spring, while turpentine bush is most commonly a fall bloomer. Together they make a great match and offer a much longer bloom. Turpentine bush can be up to 4 feet tall, but damianita is usually only about 2 feet tall. Both do best in full, unrelieved sun with light summer watering.

I love to see **chocolate flower** *(Berlandieria lyrata)* return to bloom each year. Its small yellow flowers are delightful, a wheel of yellow around a dark

Sacred datura (Datura wrightii) GARY IRISH

brown disc. It is pure fun to go out early in the morning, bend over these little discs, and savor the unmistakable aroma of chocolate. Large plantings fill the early morning with the smell.

Chocolate flower is a low plant, only 4 to 6 inches high, with numerous flowers held high above the plant. With regular irrigation, it will bloom from April through most of the summer. The receptacle, that part between the stem and the flower that resembles a flat pad, is persistent in this plant and makes a secondary green flowerlike plate for a long time after the bloom. Chocolate flower enjoys light shade and will shrink a bit in the winter, to come back beautifully in the warming days of spring.

Columbines do not seem like desert plants, but a number are native to the river ways and canyons of the region. **Yellow columbine** *(Aquilegia chrysantha)* is perhaps the best performer for the low desert garden. The first time a gardener told me he grew yellow columbine in full sun, I was positive he had it confused with some other plant, but I was wrong. This species, like nearly all columbines, enjoys a moist, rich soil and cool roots, though the tops can be in full sun. Intriguingly, it grows and blooms well in deep shade, a useful habit that makes it a good plant for many areas.

The flowers are numerous and showy, with wide-open throats of pure yellow and a stout yellow tail, or spur. Columbine will bloom for over a month in the late spring. Ranging from 2 to 4 feet tall, depending on the culture, they are astounding in a mass planting or at the back of a spring wildflower bed. The plants are biennial, so for yearly blooming it is best to establish plants two years in a row from different lots. They reseed well, and after a couple of years, you will always have columbine in your garden.

Happily, **bulbine** *(Bulbine frutescens)* is becoming better known in low desert gardens. Long, thin, succulent leaves arise from a winding woody stem that roots as it touches the ground, allowing the plant to cover an area 2 to 3 feet in diameter. Bloom begins in December and continues through the spring. The long flowering stalk opens slowly, with a few star-shaped flowers at first, then more and more as the season continues. The yellow-flowered form is most common, but there are at least two different shades of apricot in cultivation, one of which is known as 'Hallmark'. If you look at these flowers closely, you will notice the anthers are fringed in yellow, looking like small caterpillars inside the petals.

Bulbine will bloom and grow in full sun but does better in shade, particularly the apricot ones. In fact, bulbine will bloom beautifully in full shade and is a great choice for dry shade. Seeds explode all over the place, and I find little seedlings in the most interesting places—under the stairs, at the base of the redbud. When they sprout in unfortunate locations, I move them or pot them up in the fall.

Groundcovers are few in this area. Many have been tried and found unable to cope with the rugged soil and heat conditions of the low desert, but an unrivaled one for color is **sundrops** *(Calylophus hartwegii)*. Nursery people often howl at the mention of it, as it is reputed to be difficult to grow in containers, but it is worth the effort. Only 6 inches tall, it spreads 2 to 3 feet in the roughest of soils and will extend much farther in amended soils. The bright yellow, primroselike flowers occur in the spring and the fall and often intermittently in the summer, depending on rainfall. My personal favorite is a plant in my front garden that has wound itself around a black dalea *(Dalea frutescens)*, covering the newly emerged leaves in the spring with yellow flowers. In the fall the yellow flowers perfectly complement the dense indigo flowers of the dalea.

Other yellow-flowered groundcovers include **Baja primrose** *(Oenothera stubbei)*, a species that resists my efforts but looks wonderful in other gardens. A big, bright yellow bloomer, it despises being overwatered and will spread aggressively if happy. Precisely the opposite in habit, **prairie primrose**

(Oenothera missourensis) requires shade and, in fact, does well here in deep shade and will set its buttery yellow flowers all summer.

Dalea capitata is fairly new to low desert horticulture, and I have seen mixed results with it. In the Tucson area it can be a lovely late summer and fall bloomer. The yellow is clear and bright, and against its green foliage the effect is delightful. This species has the tiniest of leaflets, making it delicate and fragile looking. The plant is small, rarely over 10 inches tall, but will spread 2 feet or so. It is used as a groundcover in areas where it does well.

In the lowest desert regions it appears to do best in partial shade or a cooler spot. It often has trouble getting started in the lower desert, so extra water through the summer is a good idea. Plants rarely last long in the full sun.

Lavender cotton *(Santolina chamaecyparissus)* is well known throughout the world in temperate and dry climates but is something of a sleeper in low desert gardens. Readily available, lavender cotton is nevertheless not used as frequently as its great hardiness would warrant. The plants thrive on full sun in rocky, lightly amended soils and can tolerate a sparse summer watering schedule. Excellent drainage is a must, and in areas with ample summer rain, sharp drainage is required to keep the plant from rotting out in the summer.

Tall, slender stems hold the tiny, bright yellow buttons of bloom high off the plant in the spring. These should be pruned following the bloom, and the plant itself can be pruned or shaped at the same time or in the early fall. This soft, gray plant grows tight and compact, making it a great complement to fuller, leafier plants. It can also serve as a small hedge or border plant or as a tenacious soil builder on a rough hillside. It rarely reseeds and is grown from divisions.

Angelita daisy *(Hymenoxis acaulis),* a relative newcomer to the low desert garden, is winning me over with its dense, compact form and bright yellow, long-lived flowers. It blends well with other tight, hard shapes, such as lavender cotton, turpentine bush, and bush morning glory. It is showing itself to be tough, and roadside plantings of this species around Phoenix are doing well.

Plants are small, rarely over 6 inches high, compact, and feel hard to the touch. This species thrives in full sun in the desert. Numerous daisylike yellow flowers are held high above the plant and last from February until May. The flowers on some individuals continue nearly all year, and others bloom again in the fall. Like so many desert perennials, Angelita daisy does not like abundant water in either the coldest part of winter or the hottest part of the humid summer season. It must have excellent drainage.

Throughout the spring and early summer, the yellow flowers and dusky foliage of **desert cassia** *(Senna covesii,* formerly *Cassia covesii)* cover disturbed roadsides in the low desert. This small perennial, often grown as an annual, is a plentiful bloomer in the garden and provides excellent long-season color in hot locations. Rarely over 2 feet tall, this is a good plant for drier, less irrigated areas of the garden or for natural gardens. In good locations it reseeds prolifically, giving you plenty of seed for sharing.

When I learned that there are native hibiscus in the low desert, I was thrilled. Coming from the South, where hibiscus are used extravagantly, I began to pursue them aggressively and found that desert hibiscus are rarely grown, perhaps because they are a little difficult to grow from seed. I finally found a **Coulter's hibiscus** *(Hibiscus coulteri)* and happily put it in the perennial bed.

The first year it was a stick with nice bloom in the fall. I began to think I had overrated the entire idea until I saw what that plant did in its second and third years in the garden. Never large or full, it became a prolific bloomer year-round. It loves the sun, moderate summer irrigation, and the gentle feeding program that I give all my perennials, one good application of composted manure or compost in February and one in September.

The flowers of Coulter's hibiscus feel like crepe and are the rare clear yellow that reminds me of real lemon custard. The center of the flower is maroon, which sets off the entire flower perfectly. Plants may not last more than four or five years.

I had never heard of *Hibiscus biseptus* until I saw one at a garden sale in Tucson. I bought it only because it was another native hibiscus, little realizing it is the most gorgeous of the lot. The plant itself is ordinary, 2 to 3 feet tall, but the flowers are large, well over 3 inches across, and a brilliant, satiny yellow. It bloomed all summer, but I lost the plant the following winter, undoubtedly owing to my own deficiencies as a gardener. I am looking for another one and am determined that this extraordinary desert hibiscus will become a familiar member of desert gardens in the future.

Blue- to Purple-Flowered Perennials

Someone once wrote that purple was the kindest color in the garden and that may be so, but blue must also be in the running. Easily matched with almost any other color, it can be vivid and eye-catching or gentle and soothing.

The early spring bloom of *Justicia sonorae* falls into the eye-catching category, as it absolutely electrifies a perennial planting. The color is difficult to describe; in low afternoon light it is indigo, but during the day it is a glowing purple. This metamorphosis of color throughout the day is common in blue-flowered plants and extends their appeal in the garden.

A light, airy plant that grows to 2 feet tall, with leaves that are both small and sparse, *Justicia sonorae* works best, I think, in a mass planting. The flowers are not large, but they are plentiful from late winter through spring. This species often blooms again in the fall. The plant can be cut back for shaping in the late spring or early fall.

Justicia sonorae typifies one of the paradoxes of gardening. Some species are so good at reseeding, resettling around the garden, that they become a form of benevolent weed. This justicia, certain solanums, Mexican hat, scarlet sage, bloodweed, and trailing verbena fall into this category. Wherever conditions are good, they become prolific and eventually must be weeded and culled from places they do not belong. They won't germinate outside good garden conditions, a habit that spares them the more serious label of pest species, but before you notice, the garden will be full of them.

The Arizona native *Dicliptera resupinata* was introduced to me by my dear friends the McCombs, a couple who have introduced me to countless good plants. I do not have a good common name for it, so I call it "the clip" for short. The heart-shaped leaves are lovely in their own right, having a dusky gray-green base often tinged with purple. The leaves intensify in color through the winter.

In the spring the plant is covered with small, intensely blue flowers that eventually give way to slightly inflated, heart-shaped pods that remain on the plant for months. Once the flowers are all gone and before the weather gets terribly hot, the plant can be cut back for shaping, but I really like the pods and leave them through the summer. One plant outside the dining room resembles a small dried arrangement of intricate branches and tan pods beneath the shelter of a great old creosote. I break down and prune my plants in the winter, which appears to rejuvenate them for the spring growing season.

Trailing verbena *(Verbena tenuisecta)* grows freely in my yard. It came with the place, and my garden would be a continuous carpet of this species if I did not take a firm hand with chance seedlings. It is so pretty, though, that I have to leave some to enjoy.

Finely cut leaves give the entire plant the appearance of an old-fashioned doily. Petite purple flowers form tight bouquets held at the ends of long runners. Occasionally a plant bears white flowers, and in one area I have left white and purple to live together. I have nourished the whites, even giving some to nurseries for continued propagation. It is a good white, clear and bright, and contrasts well with the dark green foliage.

Bloom begins as early as January and continues until it gets hot, in late May or early June. Then the plants dry out and nearly disappear; they can be a sorry mess at this time if they are not cut back severely and cleaned out. Many of them will bloom again following the monsoon rains. This verbena is a tough perennial and will return from the root in the fall, supplemented by a crop of new seedlings.

Goodding's verbena *(Glandularia gooddingii)* can be perennial, but I find it fussy and difficult and so use it as an annual. I like the softer purple, which is closer to light lavender. The leaves are large and uncut, and the plant does not spread as aggressively as trailing verbena. This species grows effortlessly at slightly higher desert locations, such as Tucson.

Sandpaper verbena *(Verbena rigida)* is well named, as its long, serrated leaves are quite rough to the touch. The flowers, a deep purple, are packed tightly on a long, thin inflorescence. As with trailing verbena, the flowers appear in the spring and last a long time. This plant needs well-drained soil and regular supplemental water in the summer to continue growing and blooming well.

Ruellia brittoniana is one of those species that grow absolutely anywhere. There was a tenacious stand of it by the driveway at our house in New Orleans. With ample water it can be invasive, but that is rarely the case in the low desert. Numerous stems arise from the ground, bearing long, thin green leaves often touched with purple. Each stem ends with an open, dark purple flower. Despite its delicate look, this plant demands full sun and will turn leggy and become reluctant to bloom in the shade. A dwarf form known as 'Katie' was introduced by a Texas nurseryman. It has the same dark purple flowers but grows less than 6 inches tall. There is also a pink form called 'ChiChi' and an unnamed white form. I find the white to be disappointing; the flowers fade, turn brown, and then hold onto the plant too long after bloom. A good white that does not do that would be a very nice plant indeed.

I can't remember when I first saw *Poliomintha maderensis* (formerly *Poliomintha longiflora*), but it happened in both Arizona and Texas at nearly the same time. A researcher at the Desert Botanical Garden had collected and grown it for a number of years with no care under a large mesquite until a dry winter and hot summer did it in. Since that time I have grown and promoted this species everywhere I can; it is just lovely.

Delicate, trumpet-shaped lavender flowers fade to mauve and remain on the plant from May until December. Several flowers are held on the end of each stem, their weight causing the stem to bend in a graceful arch. The foliage is nearly as appealing as the flowers, being one of the countless species used in Mexico as an oregano. Brushing by it releases the strong oregano fragrance. Tolerant of nearly any soil as long as there is good drainage, this species prefers a situation away from the western sun in the summer. Summer irrigation every three to four days extends its life and its bloom. The plant can be cut back in late summer or early spring.

Desert hibiscus *(Hibiscus denudatus)*, a loose, open plant with sparse stems and intermittent leaves, grows only 12 to 18 inches tall. It is, however, generous with its pale lavender flowers from early in the spring until just before Thanksgiving. Easily buried by more aggressive plants, it fares best at the edge of a planting where the sun is intense and the competition somewhat reduced. I have not found it fussy about soil or watering, although it is winter deciduous.

So common as to be banal, **rosemary** *(Rosmarinus officinalis)* grows profusely in the desert garden. It is so tough that regular watering will kill it. Rosemary offers a lesson in the utility and management of Mediterranean plants in this area. As a rule, if Mediterranean natives tolerate heat at all, they tolerate it well. And as another general rule, like so many desert natives, they are adverse to too much water in the summer. This does not mean no water at all, but it does mean much less than for leafier perennials. Mediterranean species also require good, rocky drainage. Grown under these conditions, they are effortless and do not become overgrown or develop the hideous dead zone in their middle that is common in overwatered rosemary hedges.

The flowers are variable and occur in shades from deep indigo to pale lavender, depending on the variety. There are also rose-pink and white forms. Blooming takes place in late spring and early summer.

Salvia clevelandii has earned a reputation in the low desert as a tough perennial that can take dry, hot situations. Ironically, the plant usually sold as *Salvia clevelandii* is a hybrid of *Salvia clevelandii* and a hybrid cultivar. Regardless of its breeding, it is a lovely, vigorous plant for the low desert.

Generally 3 to 4 feet tall and as wide, with ample supplemental water it can grow to twice that size. Overgrown plants become floppy, heavy with too much bloom, and lose the pungent aroma and whitish blush to the leaves that make *Salvia clevelandii* such a valuable ornamental. Overwatering can also shorten the life of these plants, causing them to last less than four years. Deep, rich blue flowers are held in small whorls on 4- to 6-foot stalks. Blooming can occur anytime from March through June.

The other great blue salvia of desert gardens is **Mexican wooly sage** *(Salvia leucantha)*. These plants, which grow 3 to 4 feet tall, have dusky gray-green foliage on whitish stems that form a dense, full plant quickly. Long, fuzzy flowers occur in the spring and even more prolifically in the fall. There is a lot of color variation in the bloom, ranging from a pale lavender to a deep, saturated purple. Many salvias are short-lived perennials, and this one rarely lasts more than five years, but new plants grow quickly.

Every year Mexican wooly sage abandons the stems that bloomed that year and regenerates new ones from the base. In early summer this gives the plant a multilayered look that I enjoy. But soon the older stems begin to fade, fall over, and look tired. That is time to get rid of them and allow the next generation of stems to fill out; they are the ones that will bloom the following fall. This cycle of stem growth, bloom, and stem replacement is common in salvias, and removing the older stems encourages better form and much better bloom.

A purple aster known as **Rodney's aster** has been around desert gardens in Arizona for a few years. No one seems to remember exactly where this species came from, although it almost assuredly must have come from somewhere in Mexico. The great plantsman Rodney Engard, now deceased, brought it into horticulture.

Like many fall-blooming asters, Rodney's aster grows steadily through the summer from basal leaves and summons up a tall, stately bloom stalk in late summer. From that stalk hundreds of dark blue flowers open, beginning in October and continuing for about six weeks. New plants begin to show up in January and can be divided and moved at this time. Moving them at this time allows the little plants to set roots before the heat. This plant multiplies prolifically, so you will always have plenty to share, perhaps the finest memorial any good plantsman could want.

Trailing indigo bush *(Dalea greggii)* is a fine perennial for the summer because it is cooling just to look at. Coated with tiny silver leaves, the plants are shorter than 2 feet but spread over 3 feet in diameter, both by stems that take root and by seedlings that germinate under the branches. This plant does best with no more than weekly summer watering and can live on less in well-drained unamended soils. Grown too nicely, it tends to die in the center and spread too fast away from the center. Every four to five years prune it back sharply, remove old individuals, and fill in with the assorted rooted cuttings and seedlings that will surround it. This is best done from November to January.

Deep indigo flowers appear in both spring and fall, but I think the foliage is the most ornamental part of trailing indigo bush. It performs as a groundcover well but has many more uses in the garden. It makes a beautiful border along a path or ragged edge of concrete walk, providing gentle definition, or can serve as a small backdrop for more intensely colored low plants, like tidytips, baby blue eyes, or sundrops.

Closely allied to the tomatoes and eggplants of summer are the ornamental species in the genus *Solanum,* most of which are so confusing that names are nearly useless. I have one I got years ago that comes up with long, wide leaves and sets exquisite groups of azure flowers throughout most of the year. It was sold to me as *Solanum xanti,* but I do not believe that's what it is. A good friend in the nursery business began to grow some, calling them "irishii" for convenience. These plants show up in nurseries from time to time labeled "Solanum irishii." While the name was meant as a compliment, it is a mistake, and although the correct name of this plant is still unknown, I can highly recommend it as a garden perennial.

By whatever name, this solanum is a beautiful plant that sets numerous clusters of large, deep purple flowers every month of the year. It gets tall—old ones are more than 5 feet—and trains to a standard easily. It spreads by seedlings and root suckers, so be diligent about pulling out the ones that aren't needed. Nothing appears to bother this species.

Blue mist *(Ageratum corymbosum)* is a more rugged grower in low desert conditions than it looks, with its cool blue flowers densely packed into frothy heads. The plant is winter deciduous. Do not disturb it, and it will pop out unexpectedly one day in February. Ageratum blooms throughout the summer and fall. Generally 2 feet tall, it does well in plenty of sun or partial shade if the soil is slightly enriched and it is irrigated every three or four days in the summer. This species is a magnet for queen butterfly males in the late summer and fall.

More Colorful Perennials

A couple of years ago I threw down the seed of **Mexican hat** *(Ratibida columnaris)* to serve as filler in the garden while the perennials grew up. It has become one of the late spring stars of my perennial garden.

Starting as a small basal set in March, the plant rises quickly into a balloon of finely dissected leaves more than 3 feet tall. Like a cloud gathering moisture, the tops swell and expand until the distinctive flowers appear in mid-April. The plant continues to bloom profusely until the heat becomes intense.

The sunflower family is renowned for its unusual flower forms, but this one is bizarre even by that standard. The disc flowers are arranged in a column and form the crown of the hat, while gaily-colored ray flowers circle it, forming the brim. Colors range from brown to yellow to a brick-red, and the flowers may be one solid color or bicolored, depending on the strain.

I have found that it is best to be brutal with the plants once the flowers have faded. I cut them back, sometimes removing them altogether at this time. Smaller plants emerge throughout the summer and sometimes bloom in the late summer or fall. Once growth has commenced in the early spring or if there are seedlings, plants can easily be moved to other places in the garden.

I've heard a lot of scornful noise about **lantanas,** but I love them. Few plants are so tough, so resistant to the heat, and so pretty throughout the summer. It is true that in bad whitefly years these tiny, pesky insects can ruin its appearance, but the plants generally survive and, if pruned back severely and watered well, will resprout during the long fall season.

Three species are in common cultivation: *Lantana camara,* from which we get the familiar bicolored and tricolored 3- to 4-foot perennials in an array of yellow, orange, red, and occasionally white; *Lantana horrida,* large shrubs with intense orange-and-yellow flowers and rough, scruffy foliage; and *Lantana montevidensis,* from which the trailing forms, purple and white, are derived. All forms are full-sun hardy in the low desert but look best with regular summer watering. All are somewhat frost tender, but it takes a very cold winter to kill the stems. Interplanted with spring-blooming annual wildflowers, lantana's bare stems are hardly visible, and once the hot summer weather begins, they provide an outstanding dash of color in a desert garden.

The champion of perennials in the low desert is a common roadside native, **globemallow** *(Sphaeralcea ambigua).* Botanists separate *Sphaeralcea* variously, but for the gardener the differences between *Sphaeralcea ambigua, Sphaeralcea laxa,* and *Sphaeralcea coulteri* are nearly impossible to discern. Different colors are becoming more and more popular, with wondrous shades of red, lavender, white, purple, and pink being used along with the commonly found deep apricot.

Globemallow enjoys rough and rocky soils with excellent drainage and light summer watering or none at all. In rocky soils it reseeds prolifically, a trait it has not displayed in my propagation experience. Cuttings root easily, however, so a favored color form can be continued. I have long wanted to breed globemallows for color, form, and flower size because I have seen an amazing array of variations in natural populations, but this project may have to wait to be a retirement hobby. There are growers working on intergeneric hybrids and other cultivars, and I can only think they will all be exquisite plants.

Globemallow can become large, over 5 feet in diameter, and flop miserably in late bloom because of the weight of the stalk and flowers. Cutting it back severely at this time and maintaining regular watering will not only keep the plant tidy but result in repeated bloom before it gets hot in June. Globemallow is truly an effortless plant in the garden; nothing seems to bother it, no insects, diseases, drought, heat, or exposure. The plants can be watered or not, frequently or infrequently as you choose, through the summer.

White-Flowered Perennials

White is the color of the night. Luminescent white flowers are designed to draw in moths and other insects that fly at night. Serving as beacons, these brilliant flowers signal the presence of wonderful fragrances, many of which are so intense that one plant can fill a yard or patio with a sensuous blanket of aroma.

Sacred datura *(Datura wrightii,* also known as *Datura meteloides)* is one of the most effortless plants to grow. Its leaves emerge from a great underground tuber in the spring. In one season a three- to four-year-old plant will spread 3 feet wide or more, and older plants can be 6 to 8 feet wide and 3 feet tall. The soft, hairy, gray-green leaves are quite large and make an extremely attractive background planting in their own right.

The flower is an enormous 8-inch-long white trumpet with a light fragrance. Dozens of them open on a given night, a spectacle repeated throughout the summer. Because it is entirely deciduous in the winter, sacred datura makes a fine plant to mix with colorful winter-blooming perennials or annuals. Excessive winter watering will rot out the tubers, but plants can take any amount of water in the summer. All parts are poisonous, and just touching the leaves can cause a rash in some people.

The night-blooming **tufted white primrose** *(Oenothera caespitosa)* is a spring bloomer. I really like this plant but find it difficult to grow in my garden. It demands perfect drainage and supplemental water in the summer, yet too much summer water will kill it. Individual plants last about three years, but the species is a prodigious reseeder.

The plants form a rosette of large leaves that are green with red tinges. Older plants grow a short stem on which numerous small new plants develop. The flowers, which are large and papery, last only a day. At night they appear to be lighted from within, like white beacons, and attract night-flying insects, particularly hawk moths. Bloom is in February and March.

For sheer unadulterated exuberance of bloom, it is hard to rival **four o'clocks** *(Mirabilis jalapa).* I brought a pure white strain with me from New Orleans principally for sentimental reasons but have found this species to be a great desert dweller.

It is a perennial, although in a cold winter it is deciduous, returning each spring from a greatly swollen root. I usually cut the plants back severely sometime in late winter, even if they did not freeze, because the foliage begins to look tired by the end of January. The swollen root makes this plant fairly easy to move in late winter. Transplanting causes the top to wilt dramatically, but the root is what counts, and with steady watering and care, new stems will appear quickly. The plants can grow more than 3 feet tall in one season. They are equally easy to establish from seed and bloom the first summer after planting.

One of the great joys of four o'clocks is that it grows and blooms deliriously in deep shade. Individual flowers are small but numberless on the plants and emit a soft, delicate aroma on a humid summer evening. Bloom begins in late May or June and continues every evening in increasing profusion through the entire summer.

Not all whites are night bloomers. **Blackfoot daisy** *(Melampodium leucanthum)* is a day-blooming white perennial in the sunflower family. It requires an extremely hot, sunny spot where summer watering is minimal. Growing to about 2 feet and nearly as wide, blackfoot daisy is a compact plant, almost a perfect mound. Bloom occurs in the spring, sometimes repeating in the fall, and is a profusion of inch-wide white flowers with yellow centers.

If butterflies are your passion, desert milkweed and its close relative pineleaf milkweed are musts for daytime white color. **Desert milkweed** *(Asclepias subulata)* is a series of graceful stems up to 5 feet tall with tiny threads of leaves that appear only in March. Bloom begins in April and continues through the summer in an uncertain succession. The flowers are complicated coronets of white-cream horns. The fruit is remarkable and indicative of the family, a pair of long, sharp-tipped pods that look for all the world like mounted longhorns. They crack open suddenly, revealing a silk bed speckled with black flat seeds. Each seed is attached to a silky appendage, so that, out of the pod, it can float on the wind, giving the plant a wide range of possible new sites.

For best performance, grow this species rough. Hot, dry, well-drained sites with only intermittent summer irrigation are best. Plants get leggy, floppy, and prone to root rot if grown with too much irrigation. Aphids are fond of the branches in the late spring but rarely affect the overall health of the plant. They can be removed by hand or with a strong jet of water.

Pineleaf milkweed *(Asclepias linaria)* has small, thin, dark green leaves so fine they resemble pine needles. The plant grows 3 feet tall and has an open, loose arrangement of upright stems. The flowers are somewhat whiter than those of desert milkweed and are collected in much larger groups. Pineleaf milkweed requires full sun and sharp drainage but will tolerate partial shade in the low desert. It is from slightly higher regions of the desert and benefits from summer irrigation every three to four days.

Asclepias albicans is a large relative of desert milkweed found in western Arizona and southern California. It can reach 8 feet tall in good culture, and the stems are over twice as thick as those of desert milkweed. The stems are covered with fine hairs, making them almost pure white. This species is a stunning addition to any planting, thanks to its sculptural look and fine white color.

Buckwheat *(Eriogonum fasciculatum)* flowers are actually white, although many are fooled into believing them to be pink or red. In fact, the nearly invisible flowers are held in a tight head with each flower surrounded by a bract. It is the bract that is pink or red. These bracts are persistent for a long time after the bloom quits, giving the plant a fiery rose glow long after blooming.

One of a group of tough native perennials, buckwheat grows well in dry, rocky, unamended soils in the low desert. It grows slowly with minimal summer watering but can be encouraged to grow faster with deep watering two to three times a month. Like most native perennials, buckwheat needs winter watering for good growth and good bloom, and if it doesn't rain, the plants should be watered at least twice a month in the winter.

Desert gardeners often neglect the importance of a unifying feature or planting. It is common to see a nice selection of desert plants in a yard with nothing uniting them, with no base to the planting. Buckwheat is a species, like brittlebush or creosote, that can provide that base. Best used in quantity, it will, as the Vulcans say, live long and prosper, reseeding and settling in over the years.

A local native of the lower desert regions, *Plumbago scandens* is truly a plant for any garden and any season. Graceful white flowers can arise at almost any time but are most prolific in spring and fall. However, the real beauty is in the leaves. Green leaves envelop this 2- to 3-foot-tall rounded plant through the warm season. In winter the leaves turn a deep wine red and hold that color well into the spring. It is common for the plant to bloom at the same time these intense red leaves appear, creating a stunning effect and an unusual color combination. Prune this plant once or twice a year to keep it well shaped; with weekly watering it will grow continuously.

Late in the summer a fine cobweblike coating appears on the leaves and stems of plumbago. This powdery mildew is harmless, never diminishing the plant or retarding the bloom or otherwise causing problems, so I just leave it alone. In a few weeks it disappears.

Years ago I acquired a *Pavonia hastata*, chiefly because it was a pavonia and I was in the throes of young love for the genus. I was growing *Pavonia lasiopetala* at the time, a plant I still like for its delicate pink blossoms. For the first few years *Pavonia hastata* was a trial: it flopped and grew at odd angles, lanky and awkward. I was unsure whether this plant had a long life ahead of it in my garden, but the flowers saved it. Bright white with a wine-colored center, the 1- to 2-inch-wide flowers bloom throughout the entire warm season. Interestingly, the plant sets bud in early April, but the flowers do not begin to open until June; in fact, it must be well over 100°F before they open.

At first I adjusted to the plant's awkward growth habit by allowing a couple of seedlings to grow up in a dense planting of autumn sage, and that was lovely. The bright white flowers bloomed all summer in contrast to the deep green foliage of the salvia, and there was no need to even see the pavonia's growth habit. Lately, however, I have tried another tactic: pinching back the new growth in February and pinching often for the next month or so to fill out and form a more rounded habit. By early April the plant is a nice, neat bundle of dark green leaves with abundant flower buds.

I cannot remember why I bought *Justicia adhatoda,* but when I found out that it originated in Ceylon, I was sorry that I had wasted my money on a plant that seemed sure to fail. I was wrong, because it has proved to be a sterling plant in the garden.

Tall, over 5 feet, with long, wide leaves, this is an outstanding species for a shady spot, one with bright light but no direct sun. Numerous herbaceous stems come from the base, and each ends in a long cluster of white flowers. Individual flowers are large, over an inch long, and resemble the tail of a shrimp. The plant grows vigorously in hot weather and, if necessary, can be cut back anytime it is hot. Somewhat frost tender on the leaves, it can be pruned severely in late winter.

I have been working on **white sage** (*Salvia apiana*) so long that I think of it as the Moby Dick of my plant-growing life. Someday I will figure out how to grow this species to full size from seed. It is simply magnificent, and I want the world to have it. The only seedling I have ever brought to maturity is in front of the sales greenhouse at the Desert Botanical Garden, where it blooms and grows wonderfully.

A large plant, easily 4 feet or taller and as wide, this salvia has white foliage that is beautiful all by itself. But in late March and April, towering flower stalks, up to 6 feet tall, rise from the plant to hold whorls of white flowers. The plant needs occasional summer watering, and like brittlebush, its leaves curl and become even whiter in the summer but revive with the return of fall temperatures.

White-Leaved Perennials

All that's white in the garden is not flowers; there are good perennials grown just for their white to silver foliage. One of the most common in gardens throughout the world is the Arizona native *Artemisia ludoviciana.* Known to gardeners mostly by its cultivars, 'Silver Queen' and 'Silver King', this species is a valuable addition to a desert garden.

Grow it with too much water and it will become enormous; less water will keep it in better scale for most gardens. Like many artemisias, it is dormant in the winter, which makes the cool season a good time to transplant or relocate the plant. Just do not expect it to start growing again until the early spring. A heavy pruning in early spring not only invigorates the plant but also prevents the lanky overgrowth so common in artemisias in the summer.

Another white-leaved perennial, *Poliomintha incana,* is native to higher elevations in Arizona but does remarkably well in low desert gardens. The plant has numerous stems from a short, woody base and grows 2 to 3 feet tall. The leaves are fine and thin and range in color from light silver to pure white. Tiny white flowers bloom from late March to June.

One of my dogs has trampled this plant nearly to extinction more than once, and it has recovered immediately. So I never need to prune it for shape, but for those without canine assistance, a good pruning once a year will help keep the plant in good shape.

6 *Wildflowers and Other Annuals*

I come from central Texas, one of the few places in the world that can rightly claim to have stupendous displays of wildflowers on a regular basis. Following an arc from Corpus Christi through the rolling coastal prairies north to San Antonio, then continuing north in a wide swath nearly to Fort Worth, the spring bloom of annuals is wondrous in a mediocre year and positively unimaginable in a very good year. Acres upon acres of flowers erupt in pastures, meander along roadsides, and rise into the hills in seemingly endless arrays. Some fields are dominated by the indigo blue of bluebonnets *(Lupinus texensis)*, others by the magenta of winecups *(Callirhoe involucrata)*, and all are punctuated by the deep green of evergreen oaks *(Quercus virginiana)* and the sharp limestone edges of the hills.

Consequently, I was a bit underwhelmed by the first wildflower display I saw in Arizona. I kept my peace as everyone around me was enthusiastic, but to me it seemed spotty and localized. Individual flowers were marvelous, but as a grand display it was a little pale. And then I witnessed a pretty good year, the kind of year when the entire north face of South Mountain Park was smothered in Mexican gold poppies—you could see the color five miles away—the kind of year when the long dirt drive into the Maricopa Mountains threads through creosote flats underlaid with a seamless sea of purple owl's clover.

It clarified how different desert wildflowers are. They are beautiful, of course, but they are unreliable and fitful, subject to the great vagaries of the desert climate. In this region a really good year is a special treasure because it may not return for a decade or more; it should be savored.

Annuals in the Garden...

In gardens, however, you can improve the odds. Using wildflowers and other annuals generously, no matter how young or old the garden, creates depth and adds interest. No other group of blooming plants weaves such a rich tapestry of color into a garden scene.

Annuals are the seasonings in a garden. They can liven up mundane arrangements, fill in unexpected or temporary gaps, and add dash and vigor to a newly planted area. By nature, annuals are fast growing: germinating, maturing, and setting flower and fruit in just one growing season. There are countless uses for annuals in desert gardens, as well as a large suite of species from which to choose.

Planting, Watering, and Thinning...

Most annuals in the low desert region, whether they are native to this area or not, germinate best in the fall and winter and bloom in the spring. Even those species listed in national catalogs as summer-growing or full-sun species or those rated for the hottest areas generally grow best in the low desert during the long, cool season from September to April. Almost all annuals bloom in the low desert from February to April, a few on into May if it is a particularly cool spring.

The warm days of October are the ideal time to plant annuals in the low desert. Day temperatures are still warm, and night temperatures have started to drop. Most spring-blooming annuals germinate best when night temperatures are in the sixties; those that bloom later in spring usually germinate later in winter, just as the soil begins to warm up.

Annuals that are not from desert regions grow best and bloom most heartily in soil enriched with compost, mulch, or other organic matter. If it is possible, lay these amendments on top of the ground to a depth of 4 to 6 inches and then turn them into the ground. If that is not possible, lay on the amendments and rake them in as well as you can.

Desert wildflowers generally need much less amendment of the soil in order to grow and bloom well. Prepare the soil by running a heavy rake over the surface in one direction. Add a light layer of mulch or compost. Rake in the opposite direction to work the amendment gently into the soil. If the soil has never been worked before or is extremely hard, add more amendment and cut into the soil a little deeper.

The first time I planted annuals, mostly native species, I was deeply chagrined at their paltry germination. I had planted them in the front yard among creosote, saguaro, and ocotillo and looked forward to the rich scene I would be creating outside my dining room window. But ten poppies and forty lupines later I was a bit disturbed. Friends had wonderful displays and my neighbor had a virtual sea of color, so what was I doing wrong? Just how hard could it be? I found the answer in rocks.

I discovered that the gardeners who grew the best displays had done one of two things: turned the entire bed over and over and over again until the ground looked like a prairie or incorporated a light layer of small rocks on the surface of the soil. Known locally as quarter-minus dg (decomposed granite),

California poppy (Eschscholtzia californica) MARY IRISH

this or any similar gravel vastly improves the survival and success of annuals in this area. I wasn't interested in the plowing solution, but the rocks were definitely possible.

Plant any annual by spreading the seed on the surface of the bed. Mix tiny seed with sand or mulch to achieve a more even distribution. Cover lightly with mulch or a mulch and soil mix, using the flat edge of the rake to smooth it over the seeds. If adding dg, rake it on top. If you have existing dg in the bed, just scrape the surface with a rake, plant the seed, add mulch if you care to, and rake the dg back into place. It is not necessary to remove the stones when planting over existing dg mulch; merely raking them will be sufficient.

Water the area immediately after planting. Annuals planted from seed need to be watered every day until they germinate. Once the seeds germinate, water them every other day until the seedlings have grown five true leaves or the plants are 1 inch tall or more. Gradually extend the days between watering until the plants are being watered once a week in cold weather, twice a week any other time. Watch them carefully at this time and do not allow them to become stressed from lack of water.

After the seeds germinate in late October and November, they grow quickly to a small size and then appear to stop. They will remain virtually the same size until the first warm days of late January or early February. At that time they will begin to grow rapidly, so that within three to four weeks most will be in bloom.

Thinning is a necessary practice in broadcast plantings of annuals. It is hard to be brutal enough to do it right. Grown too tightly together, plants become stunted and weak and fail to bloom well. It is much better to be firm with yourself and get into the bed early, sometime in November or December, and pull out enough small plants to give the survivors enough space. As a rule, plantings do best when at maturity the individuals' edges touch with just a slight overlap. So for a species that will ultimately be about 4 inches across, thin the young plants to be 2 to 3 inches apart. It takes a strong heart and trust in the plants, but it will make for a great display later in the spring.

During their late-winter growth spurt is a good time to fertilize the plants if you care to. A light hand with fertilizer is advisable: too much too often will result in loads of leaves and few flowers, particularly with desert annuals.

Container Plantings...

For gardeners who have little or no space, growing annuals in containers is an easy way to add color and variety to a patio or porch. Any size pot will do, as long as it will accommodate the roots and plants when full grown. Fill with good potting soil that drains well. If desert wildflowers are used, be sure that the mix is not too rich.

Annuals in pots need to be watered regularly, every day when it is warm. In addition, a light application of all-purpose fertilizer about once a month helps the plants maintain good health and bloom steadily. Best of all, when one group is beginning to fade, another can be planted right in the same pot to keep continuous bloom throughout the year.

Collecting Seed...

I find that right after the plants have bloomed and while they are setting seed is one of my favorite times to enjoy annuals. They are prolific seed setters, producing a wonderful variety of seed and seed carriers. This is the time to save seed from any plant that had a special color or shape. If you are lucky, that characteristic will be held tightly enough in the genes to show up again and again in the garden.

If you plan to save seed, let it ripen completely on the plant. In most cases this takes about a month after bloom, and during this time some of these plants can look very messy. Take heart—it won't last long and the seed is worth it.

Once the seed is ripe, collect it by bending the seed head into a paper bag and cut it off. Leave the seeds in the paper bag or in a dish for a few days to be sure they are completely dry before being stored. Never dry or store seeds in plastic bags, as they will rot.

Seed can be stored in airtight containers in the refrigerator for a season or two, on the shelf in a cool room for a season or two, or in the freezer for a somewhat longer time. How long seed is viable depends on the species, but the seed of most desert annuals is viable for at least three years, for some much longer.

Annual Choices...

There are so many annuals it is hard to know where to start describing them. I urge experimentation. A neighbor who is a fine gardener told me she had planted scabiosa this past winter. I was aghast because I think of this species as the essence of cool, coastal summers, but they were glorious, in full bloom through April from a fall planting. Catalogs are ablaze with what are described as summer annuals in their spring issues. That is not the right time to plant them in the low desert, but many of the species listed for temperate summers are worth planting in the fall for the long, cool growing season.

Annuals are frequently known collectively as wildflowers, a nebulous term that generally means naturally occurring species within a given region and, frankly, can include both annuals and perennials. Many so-called wildflowers are sold in mixes, selected either by color or by suitability for a certain region. Mixes can be deceptive and may contain species from all over the world. It is not uncommon for a mix labeled for use in the southwestern United States to contain not only southwestern natives but species from Africa, the Midwest, and the Gulf Coast.

Sometimes it doesn't matter because a colorful array is the goal. Other times and for other uses it is important or desirable to know exactly what you are getting. Look carefully at the label and be sure that all the named species are what you want.

Spring Annuals

For most gardeners in the desert, **Mexican gold poppy** (*Eschscholtzia mexicana*) and its close relative California poppy (*Eschscholtzia californica*) are the

Painted spurge (Euphorbia heterophylla) MARY IRISH

essence of desert annuals. Both are truly beautiful flowering plants with thin petals ablaze with color in the early spring afternoon.

Mexican gold poppy is the species seen most frequently in masses on the hills and mountains of southern Arizona and is fairly easy to grow from seed. It demands full sun, and the rock mulch of decomposed granite greatly aids its success. This species usually grows 4 to 6 inches tall and bears deep gold flowers in February and March. Although it may reseed in some gardens, it is best to save the seed and add more seed to it each year until a large seed bank is built up in the soil.

California poppy is a bigger, bolder plant, usually with bright yellow-gold and occasionally white flowers. Numerous color selections are offered in the trade, ranging from mauve to orange-red and from pure white to bicolored cream in the 'Ballerina' and 'Thai Silk' series; there are also single-color cultivars, such as 'Milky White' and 'Red Chief'. California poppy is tolerant of most soils and conditions but will do better in the richer soil of an amended bed than Mexican gold poppy. Gold and white strains of California poppy reseed, but the cultivars are poor reseeders and need to be planted every year.

Lupine (*Lupinus sparsiflorus, Lupinus arizonicus,* and others) occurs regularly on roadsides in the low desert region but can be cantankerous in a garden. Some years it is resplendent; other years, reluctant. Many people swear by the practice of soaking lupine seed the night before they plant it, and this probably works, but I am much too disorganized to remember to do it.

I have tried a few lupines from other regions and can't get them to work for me, but for real presence, the incredible *Lupinus succulentus* is the one to grow. This species grows over 3 feet tall and produces huge heads of blue flowers in the spring. Despite its bulk, it is an annual and is excellent in larger beds, richer soils, or wherever you want mass and color rather than a naturalistic planting. For best performance, this plant needs to be kept well watered in the spring.

Owl's clover *(Orthocarpus purpurascens)* is a charming species, low to the ground and a luscious pink-mauve color. I think it should be planted where you can touch it, because the long spurs surrounding the tiny flowers that provide most of the color feel like the back of a baby's neck. I have never figured out the origin of its common name—not much about the plant suggests either owls or clover—but it is quite lyrical nonetheless. This, too, is an annual with its own mind and will be full and vigorous in some years and sparse in others.

The bluest blue I have ever seen is that of **desert bluebells** *(Phacelia campanularia).* This also is one of the most reliable and durable of the desert annuals. Desert bluebells will grow out of the crack of a rock, in a mixed perennial bed, in garden soil or rough native soils, with or without regular watering, and in either full sun or partial shade. Plants grown with more water and in richer soil can reach 12 to 15 inches in height and bear numerous flowers; grown less lushly, the plants are 4 to 6 inches tall but still muster great flowers.

The intense blue flowers last for three to four weeks, but I find the crinkled blue-gray foliage tinged with purple just as attractive. Once this species is in the yard, it is there forever, reseeding aggressively. I encourage it and thrill to see those tiny quilted leaves every November.

The first time I saw **five-spot** *(Nemophila maculata)* I thought it was an aberration. A tiny plant, rarely more than 4 inches tall, it has flowers with five white petals, each of which has a dark purple spot at its base. I think five-spot works best in a great mass with a few brighter-colored flowers as accent.

Baby blue eyes *(Nemophila menziesii)* is the pastel blue relative of five-spot. This species also works well in mass or in a planting to be viewed up close. I like this species in mixed potted displays as well. The plants are short, 4 inches tall, and like five-spot can be grown in either full sun or light shade.

Bladderpod *(Lesquerella gordonii)* is a low-growing yellow-blooming plant that makes a tidy groundcover for taller or brighter annuals. This is one of the earliest annuals to bloom but stays in bloom through the spring. This species will grow in full sun or light shade and tolerates the entire range of desert soils. In some places bladderpod reseeds well, but most of the time it needs to be replanted annually.

Golden fleece *(Dyssodia pentachaeta)* is sold frequently as a nursery plant and can also be directly sown from seed. The plants are small and compact, 5 to 6 inches tall, and bear prolific small yellow flowers, giving the overall effect of a planted bouquet. If these plants are happy in the garden, they will become a golden groundcover.

I do not remember if I fell for **tidy tips** *(Layia platyglossa)* because of its darling name or its precious flowers. I really like this species, especially as a low edging for a bed or with a mixed planting in a pot. The flowers are yellow with a white tip, and the petals are slightly notched. The plants are low, usually no more than 4 to 5 inches tall, and prolific. This is one of those obliging species; when you spread seed, every single one of them germinates, leaving you with the happy problem of thinning.

Farewell to spring, also known as godetia *(Clarkia amoena),* is one of the two or three annuals that I cannot ever do without. Its common name reflects the fact that it blooms late in the desert spring, beginning in late March, just as the others are fading away. The flowers bloom in an array of pink, red, purple, and white. The plants are 6 to 8 inches tall, and the flowers are 1 inch across. This desert annual is tolerant of a wide range of soils and sunlight, but appears to bloom best if grown in a slightly enriched bed.

Painted spurge, also called wild poinsettia *(Euphorbia heterophylla),* can come into bloom anytime in the garden but is most welcome in my garden when it blooms in the fall. This Arizona native produces the tiny yellow and white flowers of the genus, surrounded by showy red bracts, and is indeed a miniature poinsettia. I have never planted this annual: it just crops up in any place at any time. When it first emerged in my garden, it was a fall bloomer, but now it is present somewhere all year round. Like its hefty cousin, this species can be cut and brought into the house, where it will last as a cut flower for more than four weeks.

Scarlet flax *(Linum grandiflorum* 'Rubrum') is not a native of North America but is a superb annual in the low desert nevertheless. It grows quickly to 3 feet tall under good conditions, and the dark scarlet flowers open over a long time and can bloom from late February through early April. In mass this species makes a dramatic splash of color in a spring garden. I find that it reseeds moderately well, but replanting assures a full stand of flowers.

Toadflax *(Linaria maroccana)* is the kind of annual that I would give children to encourage them in gardening, as it is absolutely guaranteed to grow. Plants grow 5 to 8 inches tall, depending on conditions, and bloom in an array of colors—purple, pink, red, mauve, lavender, white, and yellow—some flowers all in one color, some in multicolors. Tolerant of a wide range of soils and forgiving of casual watering schemes, toadflax is a long-season bloomer in the spring. While it reseeds itself well, it is best to replant it once in a while to maintain the best variety.

African daisy *(Dimorphotheca sinuata)* is a species of mixed messages in the low desert. An annual from southern Africa, it is one of the most reliable, as well as the earliest, of all annuals for the low desert garden. It tolerates any kind of soil and any kind of watering and blooms extravagantly in hot oranges, vivid golds, yellow, and white. It reseeds itself extremely well, rarely needing to be replanted once established in the garden.

But this very extravagance calls for caution. This species easily becomes a pest and may grow where it is not wanted or needed. I have seen African daisies in South Mountain Park and growing in hot, unirrigated alleys, and once I found one in bloom on a trail in the Superstition Mountains fully 3 miles from the trailhead. While they are lovely in the urban core, this annual should not be planted in any garden that is near a park, a preserve, or a wilderness area.

Every year my neighbor's front bed, which faces south, is an intense cascade of **nasturtium** *(Tropaeolum majus)* by mid-February, while my nasturtiums, in a north-facing bed, do not begin until mid-March but continue until May. These different beds vividly demonstrate the effect of sunlight on annuals. Annuals are, with rare exceptions, plants for the full sun, the more the better. Because all of them are on a fast track to blooming, the winter sun is never too much for them. Planting annuals in too much shade may cause them to grow insufficiently, bloom poorly or not at all, and become a terrible disappointment. Most are not as tolerant as the sturdy nasturtium.

Nasturtium is not native to North America but has been with us a long, long time. Thomas Jefferson grew nasturtiums at Monticello at the turn of the nineteenth century. His were the old rambling vines, giant crawlers that run along the ground or a trellis in a riot of dark brown-reds, yellow, gold, and orange. These are still my favorite. There are now countless cultivars, not only in a wider range of colors but in more variety of form. Nasturtium is more than pretty—it tastes good. Both flowers and leaves are edible, having a pleasant crispness and a distinctive peppery aftertaste. It is best to eat the leaves when they are young because they become pepper hot when they are old.

When I first obtained seed of the old-fashioned nasturtium from Monticello, I carefully saved all the seed my plants produced. I wanted so much to maintain that old variety in all its riotous colors. I could have saved myself the trouble, though; the plants have reseeded themselves perfectly every year, with no effort on my part. Now I save the seed only to share.

The star of my annuals is **corn poppy** *(Papaver rhoeas)*, also known as Shirley poppy or Flanders poppy. It is of Mediterranean origin, as are most members of this genus, and does exceptionally well in low desert soils and climate. This species requires virtually no soil amendments to become established, a fact that has made it both useful and gorgeous in my garden. I plant it in newer beds for two to three years to help build up and enrich the soil. It rewards me a thousand times over.

The plants are usually 2 feet tall, sometimes taller, with the flowers at the tip of each stem. Like all poppies, the large flower bud nods over on the slender stem as it develops. It is a wonder how such a thread could hold this huge bud. Overnight the bud stands erect and opens, throwing its scarlet arms wide open, inviting the bees of the world to the banquet within its petals. Many forms have dark, nearly black nectar guides at the base of the petal. Flowers last only a day, but a planting will be in bloom for two to three weeks.

As the flowers fade and fall, they leave behind the exquisite urn of seed. The pods of poppies are just as ornamental as the flowers. Shaped like a cup, the capsule is topped by a colonnade of small holes topped by a fluted canopy. The seeds are minuscule and profuse, and a teaspoon will grow thousands of plants. I have had excellent germination success with this species, and it reseeds somewhat in the beds.

Ten years ago my sister gave me some seed of **bread poppy** *(Papaver somniferum)* from her yard. It took me five years to get around to planting them, and I just threw them on the ground because I wasn't sure if they were still any good. That turned out to be just the right thing to do, because this species grows best in the roughest native soil with minimal or no enrichment.

The plant is large, well over 3 feet, with floppy, cabbagelike, gray-green leaves and flowers over 5 inches across. The ones I have are purple and red, but they are available in a much wider range of colors. I mark the flowers every year to be sure to save both. Much more ephemeral than the corn poppy, this species grows for a long time but blooms for a brief time in early April.

I have not grown **hollyhocks** *(Althaea rosea)* in Phoenix yet, but those who do swear by them. Hollyhocks are really tall, 5 to 6 feet, and certain cultivars are even taller. Selection has given gardeners the entire range of color in singles and doubles. If you have the space, try them. I have decided to give them a spot against the toolshed.

Summer Annuals

Summer annuals for the low desert are a little harder to find. Although sunflower, coreopsis, and cosmos are the bedrock of summer annuals outside the low desert, here these cheerful members of the sunflower family are best planted in the fall, just like the spring bloomers, so they can come up during the cool growing season. Each of them demands full sun, but as the spring progresses, some protection from full afternoon sun will help extend the season.

Sunflower *(Helianthus annuus)* grows naturally in higher elevations of the desert Southwest and is the poster flower of high summer in the mountains. This species has an enormous natural range, over virtually all of North America, and there are numerous cultivars as a result. Sunflowers come in every size, from diminutive dwarfs only 6 inches tall to the remarkable 'Mammoth', which is more than 15 feet tall. The seed is edible, but the birds are the first to find it unless you cover or otherwise protect the head.

Coreopsis *(Coreopsis tinctoria)* is not used as much as it might be. An excellent long-season bloomer, this annual offers a blaze of yellow and brick red in striking combinations. Most other coreopsis species are worth a try in a fall-planted annual bed.

Cosmos *(Cosmos bipinnatus* and *Cosmos sulphureus)* is a finer plant, with thin stalks holding numerous finely cut leaves. The flowers of *Cosmos bipinnatus* are pink, with selections in blue and lavender as well. These plants can be large, up to 6 feet tall, and if grown in too-rich soil, can become floppy. *Cosmos sulphureus* is yellow, sometimes gold, and is smaller, up to 3 feet.

One native annual, **Arizona poppy** *(Kallstroemia grandiflora)* blooms throughout the summer on the roadsides and cutbanks of southeastern Arizona. In the lower desert it needs summer irrigation to do its best. A low, spreading plant, it can be 3 feet across and up to 6 to 12 inches tall. The flowers are a dark golden orange and shaped like a poppy, although this plant is actually in the same family as creosote. A lovely summer bloomer, it is not used nearly enough.

Another common but vastly underused annual or short-lived perennial is **purple aster** *(Aster bigelovii)*. Able to grow anywhere, the plant averages 3 feet in height and has multiple branches that bear daisylike purple flowers throughout the late spring, summer, and fall. The most prolific and well-colored flowers occur in the fall. Often spotted in waste areas, in alleys, or along fence lines, the plants look spare and lean, but when planted in mass or where they can be seen more closely, the charming purple flowers are eye-catching.

Queen's wreath (Antigonon leptopus) *GARY IRISH*

7 *Vines*

*V*ines offer a bribe: put up with their rampant, uncontrollable growth, and they will reward you with a dazzling display of gorgeous flowers.

Great sun seekers, most vines do best in the low desert with their feet planted in lightly enriched soil while their stems and flowers reach to the sun. Not all vines are traditional herbaceous crawlers. Cacti have notable vining members, especially in the genera *Selenicereus* and *Harrisia,* which do well in the low desert; *Aloe ciliaris* is a charming vining aloe with a resplendent late winter bloom; and *Xerosicyos, Ibervillea,* and *Ipomoea* are genera with vining members. Interesting as these are, however, it is the herbaceous bloomers that most gardeners seek.

Vine Choices...

Cat's claw (*Macfadyena unguis-cati*) is an exuberant, restless vine that is wildly overused in this area. *Sunset Western Garden Guide* claims that it grows to 40 feet, but I think that is conservative. It covers anything in its path and does so quickly. The flowers are bright yellow and tubular. While they are pretty, their appearance is brief, lasting only a few weeks in the late spring and followed by enormous long pods that seem to hang on forever. This winter-deciduous vine needs a hard pruning in late spring to keep it under control.

Much less perilous is **queen's wreath** (*Antigonon leptopus*). Like cat's claw, this vine is winter deciduous, although in mild areas it can retain a few leaves. A great heat lover even in the low desert, queen's wreath does need regular watering during the summer to look its best. It is quite forgiving of soil conditions, growing equally well in amended soil or in virtually untouched soil. Light falls of flowers cover the plant gracefully throughout the summer. The color is a soft, deep pink, although there is a deep red form called 'Baja Red'.

Yellow butterfly vine (*Mascagnia macroptera*), also known as yellow orchid vine, first came to my gardening attention in New Orleans at the splendid Longue Vue estate. There a small patio was devoted to yellow-flowering plants, and this vine covered one wall of the outdoor room. The color is dazzling, a clear, bright yellow, and the flowers have an unusual shape. The petals are arranged like a wheel, with thin rods of yellow petal supporting frilled spoon-shaped tips. This species blooms only in the spring.

The common name of butterfly vine is derived from its seed carriers, which are large winged pods that begin the season lime green and end it a parched shade of beige. Dried, they are elegant. Despite its short blooming season, this vine is extremely drought tolerant and heat resistant and will quickly cover a wall, fence, or arbor. It is evergreen but hardy only to the mid-twenties.

Purple butterfly vine *(Mascagnia lilacina),* also called lavender orchid vine, is more slender than its yellow relative both in flowers and leaves. The pale lavender flowers that appear in the spring, sometimes later, are a delicacy often shown to best advantage by either planting the vine close to view or interplanting it with a more vigorous partner.

Yuca *(Merremia aurea)* is a great tease. It is entirely deciduous in the winter, but in early spring distinctive three-part leaves on thin stems emerge from the plant's swollen tuber to cover a fence or arbor in a very short time. Stunning gold-yellow flowers blanket the vine throughout the hottest part of the summer. The seeds are prolific and germinate quickly in the hot weather. Because it grows from a large tuberous root, this vine is extremely drought tolerant.

Yuca is, however, still hard to find in nurseries. Frustrating to grow despite the fact that it readily germinates, yuca is tricky to transplant when small. Work continues to bring this extraordinary vine into continuous cultivation.

Podranea ricasoliana hit the Phoenix area with a bang a few years ago as a great addition to our vine flora. Brought into cultivation in Arizona from plants in Mexico, it has been cultivated in the tropics and subtropics for a long time but is originally from South Africa. It is easy to see why it has made the journey around the world of gardeners.

A loose vine with no tendrils, podranea requires a trellis or other support. It blooms in late summer and fall, reaching its peak in October with cascades of stunning bell-shaped pink flowers. This vine is an outstanding choice to cover a patio or ramada or to camouflage a hot wall. It grows well in full sun or partial shade and is not fussy about soil. Deep soaks every 4 to 5 days in the summer and much less water during the rest of the year will keep the plant growing and blooming well.

Leaves occasionally yellow in the summer and are helped by a light fertilization or an application of manure, but otherwise this is an effortless vine to grow. During its first year in the ground, podranea sits still, hardly appearing to grow. Be patient, for by the third year it will be large and bloom regularly and prolifically. It often looks ratty in the late winter but rarely loses all its leaves. Give it a hard pruning in January just as the new growth is beginning to emerge. Bloom, as in most vines, is on the new growth, so do not prune too late.

Growing vines in shade is usually problematic, but **Arizona grape** *(Cissus trifoliata)* is a terrific choice. Despite the common name, this vine does not have edible fruit but is grown chiefly for its hard, dark green foliage. Superficially it resembles ivy and, in fact, can well substitute for it (with much less water) if left to grow along the ground. Mine covers the barren trunk of a highly pruned African sumac, but it will do the same for bare dirt in a shady location.

This vine is slow to start. A 1-gallon plant may look pathetic with one tiny sprig barely reaching the edge of the pot, but it is a hot-weather grower and will become enormous the longer it is in the ground. In the low desert it is generally green all winter; plants in containers or in cool areas are entirely dormant in the winter. They recover quickly in early March, putting out aggressive growth through the warm summer months. Older plants in the ground that are well protected from the cold are rarely dormant or even deciduous.

Australian blue vine *(Hardenbergia violacea)* is a prolific vine that produces deep, intense blue-purple flowers throughout the summer. A white-flowering form exists as well. This species likes barely enriched soils, full sun, and regular water. It is a moderate- to slow-growing plant at first but with time will become a luscious full cover for a patio, wall, or gazebo. It is evergreen and rarely requires pruning except to keep it in bounds.

There are a few neglected natives to add to the vine flora of our gardens. A great favorite of mine, **passion vine** *(Passiflora foetida),* is an extremely heat- and drought-hardy species that is still difficult to find for sale. The plant crawls over fences with tenacious tendrils bearing halberd-shaped, fuzzy, gray-green leaves. The pale lavender flowers are complex, about the size of a quarter. The fruit is a small pod coated inside with a delicious slippery gel. This fruit is edible and pops delightfully in your mouth when fully ripe.

Rambling through the bushes of the mountain ranges around Arizona's cities is another good native vine, **snapdragon vine** *(Maurandya antirrhiniflora)*. Its flowers are small, less than half an inch, but prolific and look just like snapdragon flowers. The most common color is a deep, dark blue, but there is a wonderful carmine-colored form as well. Snapdragon vine is easy to grow from seed or transplant and sets so much seed that there will always be a few strays around the garden. A prolific bloomer in the hottest part of summer, this vine often dies out in winter but is replenished by the plentiful seed it drops.

Gourds are low, lazy vines that make good groundcovers. **Coyote gourd** *(Cucurbita digitata)* and **buffalo gourd** *(Cucurbita foetidissima)* are desert natives, impervious to desert summer conditions. Each can become enormous and will spread over huge runs of a large yard if given the chance. Best grown from seed, gourds require some heat and water to germinate and regular irrigation through the summer. The large yellow, squashlike flowers are followed by baseball-sized gourds in the late summer and early fall.

8 *Cacti*

Cacti are icons of the American Southwest. Wherever they are—thrusting out of rockfalls, scattered across a tranquil desert plateau, or marching up and down hills in a rhythm thousands of years old—these plants are so bizarre, inverting all prior understanding of plant life, it is no wonder they inspire awe, interest, and surprise. The care with which they must be approached, guardians of their arid space, only increases the mystique. They are achingly beautiful.

Hillsides of cholla, too thick to count, appear to move and flow in a sinuous wave, like a spiny watercourse over the dry hills. Sunsets ignite the silhouettes of saguaro, changing the green of life to the golds and reds of firelight before dissolving to black in the long desert twilight. Backlit, the golden spine sheaths of teddy bear cholla incite our imagination with reminders of spirits and shapes from a very distant past.

Cactus Features...

Flowers

Cactus flowers are among the most exquisite in the plant world, a rowdy and raucous contrast to their austere environment and the spare form of their parent plants. Their colors cover the spectrum, from shocking magenta, fiery orange, and brilliant yellow to delicate pastel shades of lavender, cream, and pink. White is predominant in night-blooming cacti, a beacon for the night-flying moths and bats that pollinate these plants. Cactus flowers can be tiny, such as those of star cactus, pincushion cactus, or Christmas cholla, or large, as in the night-blooming cereus or Easter lily cactus. Most have little fragrance, but the exceptions, such as Arizona queen of the night, which exudes its lusty perfume on only one night of the year, can dominate a garden.

Cactus flowers may be sparse, such as those of barrel cacti, or copious, like the clouds of flowers set by species of *Harrisia*, which bloom with more than a hundred 8-inch-long flowers per night. Bloom can occur once a year, as in hedgehogs, or grace the entire warm season with a scattered bloom, as in the Easter lily cactus. Flowers can ring the stem, as seen in the serene pink halo of fishhook pincushion; they can emerge up and down the rib line, as in organ

Purple prickly pear (Opuntia violaceae) **MARY IRISH**

pipe and Mexican fence post cacti; they can crowd the tip, as is common in barrels; or they can erupt from the skin, like those of hedgehog cacti.

Colorful Spines and Skin

As beautiful as they are, cactus flowers are a fleeting show. More permanent but equally stunning color combinations can be found in the spines and skin of many species. The pads of purple prickly pear are a remarkable gray-blue edged with rich, royal purple. The intensity of that purple varies considerably; new pads are often completely purple, and cold weather intensifies the color dramatically. The dense, dark green skin of the Mexican fence post takes on a classic elegance with the fine line of white bristles that mark each rib. Young *Myrtillocactus geometrizans* and many forms of night-blooming cereus are covered in a fine blush that renders the skin a charming deep blue.

The spines of firebarrel are so red they appear to be dipped in blood; the plant becomes the burning bush of the Baja when backlit by the fierce Sonoran sun. The golden sheaths of teddy bear cholla spines illuminate the entire plant in a vibrant glow. Long white bristles grace the length of old man cacti

(Cephalocereus senilis, Oreocereus trollii, Espastoa lanata), turning these plants into gentle white pillars.

Shapes

There are more than 1,500 species of cacti, all of them native to the Americas. In general, cacti come in three basic shapes—column, barrel, or jointed stems—and there are myriad variations within those shapes. Columnar cacti can be immense and treelike, such as the saguaro or cardon; large and multi-stemmed, like senita, organ pipe, or night-blooming cereus; or small with numerous stems, such as hedgehog or claret cup cactus. Barrel cacti range from the great compass barrel of the Sonoran Desert or the golden barrel so popular in this region, to the more moderate-sized horse crippler, down to the elfin genus *Frailea* of South America. Jointed-stem cacti, most familiar as prickly pear and cholla, also include the genera *Schlumbergera* and *Zygocactus,* from which the beloved Christmas cacti are hybridized.

Some cacti are difficult to characterize. The vining forms of golden torch, for example, alternately seek a shrub for support or trail along the ground, then suddenly turn to the sky and stand pole straight. The Arizona queen of the night has extraordinarily thin stems that branch and reach into creosote or palo verdes for support, mimicking dead stems as camouflage. And then there are the genera *Pereskia* and *Pereskiopsis,* relics from the ancestors of cacti, which have dark, woody stems, a shrubby form, and true leaves.

Cacti in the Garden...

Despite this suite of admirable traits, cacti have not earned a very prominent place in most desert gardens. They are too often relegated to the outer fringes of the yard or isolated among a few rocks or perhaps along a small fence as part of a "desert landscape." Cacti never occur naturally in such isolation, and rare is the garden that can achieve beauty and balance under such a Spartan regimen.

I have to ask myself, why this scorn and neglect from gardeners in the desert? Here are plants that are elegantly designed to withstand the rigors and torments of a hot, dry region, that come in an astounding array of forms and a riot of colors, and yet they occupy but a tiny portion of our gardens. I suspect that the answer lies in that oddity that makes them so fascinating. While cacti have a large and devoted following and thousands of avid collectors worldwide, for many gardeners they are strange plants that fall outside their personal gardening experience. Cacti are succulent, they have spines, their culture and care are different, and they do not commonly grow east of the Mississippi River—all of which supports the trepidation most gardeners feel about growing them in the garden.

There is a wide range of uses for cacti in the garden. What better way to set off a frothy series of perennials than with the hard, clean edge of a hedgehog or beaver-tail prickly pear? How much more interest will be created in a planting of creosote, ocotillo, and wildflowers if a well-placed cholla or barrel cactus is included to focus the view?

Cacti can serve as boundary and border plants, as well as hedges; they certainly have all the equipment to be excellent deterrents to unwanted traffic. Great bushy pereskias (*Pereskia grandiflora* and others) grace roadsides and pastures in the wet-dry subtropics of Central America. Our occasional frosts keep them to a more moderate size, but these shrubby, leaf-bearing cacti make a lovely visual screen or a daunting hedge, rewarding us with exquisite pink and purple flowers in late spring and summer.

Prickly pears, particularly the sprawling types like desert, chenille, and Engelmann's prickly pear, achieve the mass and complexity to serve as good hedges. Some chollas, like cane and staghorn cholla, are easily considered a succulent shrub and can be used as such in a desert garden. Other prickly pears, such as purple prickly pear and beaver-tail, as well as teddy bear cholla and pencil cholla, all blend well in a naturalistic garden, mingling with desert shrubs such as creosote, Texas ranger, hopbush, fairyduster, and jojoba.

You can add height to a long border of desert perennials by incorporating the columnar forms of old man of Mexico, Mexican fence post, or organ pipe into the design. By blending night-blooming herbaceous plants, such as tufted white primrose, with night-blooming Easter lily cactus, bold *Trichocereus*, or Arizona queen of the night, you can create a traditional night garden with a distinctive desert touch.

Cacti are rarely used in mass, but such a planting can have dramatic and effective results. I have seen attempts, mostly in southern California, at massing plants of *Mammillaria*, and they worked quite well. This kind of planting is not for everyone or every circumstance, but I find it exhilarating to see cacti used as something more than the ubiquitous accent plant.

An accent plant, of course, is one that serves to focus the eye or set off other plants to particular advantage, and certainly a well-placed cactus can accomplish this goal. I cringe, however, when writers and designers consign cacti solely to this category. This is like insisting that eggs are only for breakfast; it limits and defines the uses of cacti too much, rejecting further possibilities.

A bed of night-blooming cacti would be charming, especially near a patio that is used in the evening or early morning. The Arizona queen of the night is a particularly intriguing choice, with its cryptic stems and stunning, fragrant blooms. Night-blooming cereus, *Harrisia* species, and the short *Trichocereus candicans* are great favorites of mine for night bloom. The harrisias will vine and twist through a mesquite or palo verde or rise and fall on themselves if grown without support. More than eight flowers may open on a single plant, and unlike the Arizona queen of the night, harrisias repeat their blooming feat over the course of the summer.

Arranging large plants such as saguaros or cardons in a garden is sometimes difficult. Because saguaros are native and popular, they are plopped into all kinds of unusual and unsuitable settings. I have seen a saguaro placed right beside the decking of a pool, where it could fall into the pool or the roots could heave the decking; in the middle of a lawn, which receives vast amounts of water the plant cannot tolerate; beneath the eaves of a house, where it will lift the roof as it grows; and, remarkably enough, in the middle of a house with a piece of the roof cut out for it. In a successful attempt to save water but a vain attempt to look like a garden, saguaros are often planted alone in the front yard, surrounded by a sterile, sere scene of gravel and perhaps a boulder or a chain fence at the edge. To me these glorious Sonoran figureheads look better mixed with other tall plants with plenty of viewing room, where the impact is not as centerpiece but as masterpiece.

Cacti As Food...

Cacti also have a place in the vegetable patch. I keep a spineless Indian fig prickly pear in the yard specifically so I can enjoy that great cactus delicacy, *nopalitos*. The word *nopal* comes to us from the ancient Nahuatl language of Mexico and refers to a single pad or occasionally to an entire cactus plant. Spanish linguistic custom refers to the young pads as *nopalitos,* meaning little or dear *nopals.* Such charm in naming an ordinary and humble food supports the reputation of Spanish as a loving tongue. Young pads are harvested when they are pliable and tender, then peeled, chopped, and boiled briefly. After that they can be added to soups or stews, both for flavor and as a thickening agent, and are most often used with eggs. Fresh *nopalitos* have a slightly piquant flavor and make a sensational addition to fresh salsa.

The fruit of almost all cacti is edible, although there is a vast range in palatability. Saguaro fruit is so delicious and was of such importance to the Tohono O'odham people in the low desert of Arizona that their year began with harvesting this fruit in June. I like the fruit best when it has been sun-dried on the plant, which turns it into a piece of fruit leather. To get the best fruit, you have to beat out the birds and pull the fruit down. The ones that fall naturally either are unripe and bitter or are bird-ravaged hulls.

The fruit of desert prickly pear is likewise excellent and makes outstanding jelly and jam. *Pitaya* is a term in Mexico for both tall multitrunked cacti and their fruit. All are tasty and are sold in markets throughout Mexico. Candy, wine, and syrup are other common products made from a wide variety of cacti.

The truly adventuresome gourmet can roast and dry the flower buds of cholla for eating. They taste vaguely like artichoke and at one time were an important staple for desert Native American peoples. In my opinion, they are not worth the effort, but you have to respect people who knew enough to cook and eat such things in the first place.

Sun and Cold...

Many structures and features of cacti are adaptations to living in hot, dry areas where rainfall is irregular and rarely plentiful. These adaptations, all designed to minimize water loss, include a sturdy cuticle covering the skin; spines in place of leaves; few stomata, the minute openings through which water and gas exchanges take place; photosynthesis activity primarily at night so that stomata open only when it is cool; a wide, spreading root system with countless tiny root hairs that can die off and regenerate in days to absorb rainfall; and succulence, that astonishing transformation of cells just under the skin into water reservoirs that sustain the plant during prolonged periods of drought.

Despite all these adaptations, many cacti cannot tolerate the full sun of the low desert. Most small barrels, such as those in the genus *Mammillaria, Coryphantha, Echinopsis,* and *Gymnocalycium;* certain species of *Echinocereus;* as well as the tender octopus cactus and *Acanthocereus pentagonus* require light shade in this area. Golden barrels grow well in light shade but will accept full sun if slowly acclimated to it, and they achieve the brightest yellow spine color in the highest sun they can tolerate.

Cold presents its own problems for many sun-loving cacti. There are so many charming photographs of saguaros with snow on the top of them that it is easy to forget that saguaros actually are frost tender. The areas north of Phoenix in the New River Mountains and the Mazatzal Range are the northern limits of this species. Cacti such as Mexican fence post, organ pipe, and senita are even more sensitive to cold and are quite vulnerable to freeze damage in the low desert.

The first time inverted foam cups were used on the tips of the columnar cacti at the Desert Botanical Garden for frost protection, it became a media event. Photographers swarmed the Garden, grabbing the opportunity for this novel view of the collection. Those cups work extremely well and make safe and easy protection for the more than 9,000 cacti in the collection. At home I find the cups are unwieldy and must be removed within a day or so because they block so much light. For only a few plants, a frost blanket is much easier to use. You can either throw it over the entire plant or cut small pieces and tie them with tree tape to the stem. A good friend ties mini blankets of frost cloth to the tips of his columnar cacti at the beginning of winter and does not unbundle them until the danger of frost is past; his plants suffer no etiolation or other growth problems.

Watering...

Every desert gardener has been mystified by the sudden death of a favorite cactus or stunned when a large plant that was seemingly healthy suddenly collapses. How could something so well suited to this area and so precious just die? It is often the result of too little or too much water.

Most large cacti planted in the ground never need supplemental irrigation between October and March, but watch the weather; a particularly long, dry spell in the winter (60 days without rain) means the plants need a good, deep irrigation. In April, May, June, and July, all large cacti need supplemental irrigation to look their best, avoid wilting, and stay healthy. For mature plants in good condition, once a month is adequate; for smaller individuals or plants requiring a little more water, such as prickly pear, every two to three weeks is needed. August and September demand that you watch the weather; if the monsoon season is inadequate, continue with the summer watering schedule.

Cacti show their need for water dramatically. In columnar species, such as saguaro, look for a reduction in the space between the ribs; if you cannot get one or two fingers between the ribs, the plant needs water. The skin of a well-hydrated plant is resistant to touch; if it gives way when you push on it, the plant needs water. Badly desiccated plants also have wrinkled skin.

Prickly pear skin withers and puckers when the plant needs water. Arborescent (treelike) plants droop and lose rigidity as their water needs become more acute. Pale or yellowing skin is a sure sign of stress in any cactus and often occurs before the onset of wilting as an early warning signal that you need to water your plants.

Every summer before the onset of the monsoon rains, I fight a battle to keep the big Indian fig prickly pear from drooping. Wilting from lack of water happens quickly and, if allowed to continue too long, can severely affect your plant. I have found that a long, slow, deep watering will bring it back. Severe desiccation can be prevented by a regular schedule of deep irrigation. If the plant has wilted so much that the pads still droop after a good watering, it is necessary to prune at least one pad from each stem series to reduce the weight and prevent breaking and splitting.

Members of the genus *Ferocactus* are astoundingly drought resistant and able to remain healthy on rainfall alone. Two common garden cacti, the charming Easter lily and the stately night-blooming cereus, do require regular irrigation throughout the summer. Both bloom repeatedly if kept well watered.

The water needs of small barrels and pincushion cacti are harder to determine. Look for a discoloration of the skin and a shrinking look to the plant as symptoms of water stress. Small barrels and pincushions are notorious for standing as a blank shell for years after they have died, the dense coat of spines masking all symptoms of stress.

Smaller cacti look charming when used with rocks, but there are other, more practical reasons for incorporating rocks in your garden plan. The rocks cool the soil beneath, especially in the critical few inches where the plant's roots grow, and because the soil is a little cooler, it holds more moisture. These are minute but crucial differences to a cactus.

How much to water is nearly as puzzling as when to water. The wide-spreading roots of cacti fan out from the plant like the spokes of a wheel. The roots are not deep: those of a large saguaro will be only 4 feet deep, while those of large barrels and prickly pears rarely exceed 3 feet, and hedgehogs and pincushions have roots only inches below the surface. Older roots thicken and become tough while holding up a large plant, but it is in the profusion of microscopic root hairs that the action of transferring water-soluble nutrients and gases takes place. This area at the frontier of the root system is where the plant needs water. Therefore, to irrigate a plant most effectively, water in a circle around the plant and use a slow delivery, either by hose or drip system, to achieve maximum percolation.

For large columnar cacti this can mean a radius from the stem to the outside rim of the roots of up to 6 feet; a reasonable rule of thumb is to assume the roots extend outward from the plant to about half of its height. For barrels and smaller plants, a radius of 2 to 3 feet is adequate, but prickly pears can have roots running 5 to 6 feet from the plant.

Basins are an effective way to water large cacti, such as saguaro, organ pipe, cardon, myrtillocactus, or night-blooming cereus, and I find them to be a good way to slow down water so that it percolates deeply into the soil. It is important, however, that water not sit around the base of the plant for a long time. Add another low berm close to the base to prevent too much water from being in contact with the skin of the cactus.

The greatest difficulty most garden cacti face is receiving too much water on a steady basis. Cactus roots absorb moisture from the soil as long as it is available; like a teenage boy with his first beer, the cactus does not know how to quit and will eventually burst in the process. Long, longitudinal scars are a frequent indication of this condition, as is a rotted root system.

The watering needs of plants in pots vary from those of plants in the ground. The larger soil mass of the garden means that soil moisture is available over a much longer time. Moisture in the soil is constantly conducted up to the root zone by capillary action as water evaporates or is used by plants. If the ground has been well soaked or is cool, it can take a long time to critically deplete the soil moisture for cacti. In a pot, on the other hand, because all sides of the smaller column of soil are exposed to the air, it can take only days for the soil to dry out completely, especially in hot weather.

The strategy I use to determine when to water potted plants is to plunge a pencil or stick into the soil regularly, perhaps weekly. If the soil is entirely dry, water the plant thoroughly and completely. The common advice to give cacti only a tablespoon of water is bunk; you should apply water to the pot until it runs out the drain hole. Small potted plants and newly established plants may be watered weekly in hot weather. Be more careful when it is cool, because soil dries out much more slowly and plants use less water.

Transplanting...

Moving cacti, especially saguaro, has become something of a folk art in this part of the country. It is common to see these disturbed giants parked in rows along road or housing construction sites, waiting to be returned to the rocky land where they have lived for decades. There are many ways to move a cactus, but I have seen the best success and the greatest regrowth with the following method. These guidelines apply whether you are moving a plant from pot to pot, from a pot to the ground, or from one place in the ground to another.

Regardless of their size, cacti move best if their root system is dried before they are replanted. This allows all the tiny lesions that occur during uprooting to heal thoroughly before the roots are exposed again to moisture. This simple practice goes a long way toward preventing rot, so common in newly transplanted cacti.

Uprooting a cactus is the equivalent of a sudden onset of drought, a condition that, ironically, helps make cacti easy to transplant. When soil moisture reaches a critically low level, cactus root hairs begin to die, signaling the plant to switch to a metabolic drought survival mode in which metabolism slows and the plant shifts to using stored water for photosynthesis. This mechanism is a crucial adaptation for survival where rainfalls can be months apart. Likewise, it is also a highly desirable condition for transplant. Once slowed down, plants can remain out of the ground for weeks or months and can regenerate roots quickly once they are replanted and watered.

As you begin transplanting, withhold water from the plant for at least a week and then lift the plant from the ground or the pot and shake off the soil, treating the roots as gently as possible. It is not necessary to get rid of every speck of dirt unless it is terribly contaminated; a vigorous scrubbing only damages the roots.

Once the cactus is out of the soil, move it to a dry, shady location to let the roots heal. Leaving it on the ground invites rot. Also, uprooted cacti sunburn easily, so be sure the plant is out of the sun. It can be left in this condition for months if necessary, but one to two weeks is plenty. I had a neighbor who was cleaning out a closet and came over to show me the treasures she had found. In a box were three small cacti, a little shriveled but green and alive. She was uncertain how long they had been there, but it was well over a year. This was an extreme example, but once cacti are uprooted, they have the ability to live a long time out of the ground.

For large plants this drying-out practice can be difficult or impractical. In that case, lift the plant from its original location, shake off the soil, and plant it in a previously prepared dry hole. Hold off on initial watering for at least 10 days, longer if the weather is cool.

Mark one side of the plant before it comes out of the ground and reorient the plant in the same direction. Failure to do so can cause sunburn, which often leads to infections. Like ours, cactus skin is thin and easily burned, and it must acclimate to the harsh desert sun. If you do not know the original orientation, protect the south and southwestern sides of the plant with shade cloth during its first summer.

Plant cacti only as deep as they were growing in the old place. If they are planted too deep in the hole or if dirt is mounded around them, moisture in the soil will encourage the skin to rot. The Desert Botanical Garden lost dozens of saguaros in the initial plantings for the Plants and People of the Sonoran Desert trail because of the old practice of sinking the plants 3 feet into the ground. Autopsy revealed that most of those that died had developed a rot that spread from the skin to the interior of the plant, thereby creating a plug in the vascular system and starving the plant.

If the plant is so large or unsteady that it will not stand on its own, stake it as you would a tree. Attach a collar of a material that will not cut the skin, such as garden hose, and wire the collar to stakes in the ground. Use at least

Organ pipe cactus (Stenocereus thurberi) **MARY IRISH**

two stakes opposite each other and parallel to the prevailing wind; four are even better. Supports that touch the plant, such as carpet-cushioned lumber, invite rot and cause the skin to sunburn when they are removed. Staking is necessary for only three to four months; by then the plant should have established an adequate root system.

What can you do if you find yourself with a plant that was planted deeply and is not thriving? It is highly impractical to just pull out a 12-foot saguaro and start all over again. Because the roots of the plant are now deep beneath the soil surface, ordinary watering schedules and rain rarely percolate down to the root zone. Correct this by watering two to three times the normal duration to allow water to reach that extra depth. For the rest of its life the cactus will need this extra-deep watering.

If the roots have been allowed to dry before replanting, you should water the plant after transplant. If the roots have not been air-dried, then do not water immediately; wait at least a week. Incalculable numbers of large plants, especially saguaros, have died slowly and unnecessarily because they were not watered after they were moved. Transplanted plants must have soil moisture to stimulate regeneration of the root system. Water transplanted cacti well and regularly, every 7 to 10 days initially and gradually extending to every two to three weeks. Continue watering regularly for the entire first year the plant is in the ground.

Pests and Diseases...

Cacti are kind to gardeners; they have surprisingly few pests, problems, or cultural demands. For my money, the most destructive and difficult pests are rabbits. Both cottontails and jackrabbits are ferocious and persistent in their attacks on cacti. Once they have nibbled that first bite away from a spine, they are free to decimate the plants. These terrors can girdle large barrels and saguaros and are particularly ravenous during midsummer, when the desert is at its driest. Other than a good gun or slingshot, I know of no sure control.

Fencing works well with cottontails, but jackrabbits just tear it down or leap over it. Besides, a yard full of chicken wire hoops and cages is hideous or, in the case of large plants, impractical. Rabbits are one of the most vexing pests in any garden, and I am sure that I am doomed to many more late afternoons chasing these teeth on four legs down the alley.

Insect pests are rare on most cacti, but one is so interesting I find it hard to think of it as a pest. For a gardener, however, cochineal scale can pose a problem, most commonly on prickly pears and chollas. Cochineal scale comes from a minute insect, the female of which spins a tight, cottony mass around her tender, delicate body. Secluded from the sun and voracious predators in this foamy cave, the insect sucks nutrients from the plant. A small gathering of cochineal is benign, but the insects can quickly multiply and damage a plant. Direct a strong jet of water to disintegrate the protective mass. The water pressure and the exposure to the air will kill the insects. During the warm season you may have to wash the plant repeatedly to keep the cochineal under control.

The interesting fact about these insects is that the female's body is the source of a splendid red dye known as cochineal red. Touring a guest once through my yard, I squeezed the soft white ball between my fingers to show the exquisite color. My fingers turned a deep berry red, and pleased, I held out my hand for inspection and, I thought, admiration. My guest just stared at my hand and finally, in a very small voice, asked, "You mean, you just squashed the bug?" "Sure," I said, "that is what makes the dye," but as I prepared to go on with the fascinating tidbit that it was the source of the term *redcoat* in the English army, I found that she had already moved away. We never returned to the insects, and I suspect she didn't share my fascination.

Cactus longhorn beetles are insidious creatures, slyly marring any cactus they encounter. One of my columnar cacti began to have odd, eaten parts at the top. It was hard to imagine what could be responsible—the plant was tall. One evening I watched a large black bug crawl up the entire height of the plant. Fascinated, I looked closer and saw it begin to idly munch on my plant. It was a longhorn cactus beetle, easily identified by its antennae, which were the length of its body. This one was immediately decapitated with a pair of shears; I recommend you do the same. Larvae of the cactus longhorn beetle develop at the base and interior of the plant, eating out the heart. They are difficult to detect and to control.

Birds are not a pest of saguaros. Gila woodpeckers and saguaros have developed a coexistence over the unimaginable journey of evolutionary time, and all our pitiful efforts to deter the birds from nesting in saguaros are in vain. Woodpeckers come from a family of cavity nesters who prefer to nest high off the ground. In the Sonoran Desert, where tall trees are rare, the Gila woodpecker became adept at using the tallest pole on the plain, the saguaro. The saguaro over time became equally adept at insulating the great wound the woodpecker built for a nest and shutting it off so that it did not become a place of infection. The entire cavity and its protective self-sealing wrapping are known as a boot, which persists long after the death of the plant.

In the natural desert there are many saguaros and few woodpeckers. But woodpeckers love the urban environment, and there the tables are turned: there are many woodpeckers but few saguaros. This leads to overcrowding in the saguaro nesting market. Stuffing a hole to discourage the birds does nothing but jeopardize your plant, particularly if the stuffing is chemical, liquid, or holds water. Nor are saguaros improved by a veil of green netting, and I am certain that woodpeckers are only temporarily deterred by such raiment. The woodpecker, after all, has a strong need to nest and cannot be dissuaded or frightened from the idea. It is better just to relax, consider nesting woodpeckers one of the privileges of your garden, and enjoy them.

Saguaro rot, or bacterial necrosis, is a vexing problem for gardeners. This infection can be set off by a wide variety of problems: sunburn, injury, frost damage, too much water, or poor drainage. The bacteria travel through the vascular system of the plant, frequently becoming widespread before the plant shows external symptoms. Those symptoms are dramatic and definitive: the plant will ooze a black liquid that smells bad; there may be open wounds in the skin; and the plant may lean. If the oozing occurs low on the cactus, the plant is probably not salvageable and should be removed if it might fall on people or property. If rot occurs at the tip of an arm or the tip of the cactus, cutting off the infected area may offer some hope. Wipe the wound with a diluted bleach and water solution, let it dry, and hope.

Cactus Choices...

Columnar Cacti

You cannot move in southern Arizona without bumping into a photograph, carving, or painting of **saguaro** *(Carnegiea gigantea)*. This is fitting tribute to one of the wonders of the botanical world, a cactus so large that it is tree, a plant so huge that it can provide multiple nests for hawks, owls, thrashers, and woodpeckers, as well as snakes, rodents, and an unimaginable array of insects.

Saguaros stand over 50 feet tall at maturity, and most of them grow a number of branches, known as arms. There is great debate over what induces a saguaro to make arms. Most plants are 10 to 12 feet tall before they begin to grow arms, and under natural conditions that could mean they are up to 75 years old, but the individual variation is fascinating. Some saguaros have dozens of arms, others just a few, and occasionally one will reach full mature height with no arms at all.

In May and June a corona of large white flowers blooms at the tips of the central column and arms. Although the flowers open at night, they remain open long into the morning. The flowers are followed by large red fruit that tastes delicious, not just to me but to all desert creatures.

All columnar cacti are held up by a frame of layered tissue called wood. Cactus wood is hollow and has numerous holes and fissures. Like the struts of a bridge or the bones of a bird, it is delicate and light but strong. This column of wood surrounds each stem and is somewhat star shaped in cross section. Each "point" in the star marks the line of a rib. Once covered with skin, this ribbing affords the plant the flexibility to swell when there is plenty of water and shrink when water supplies are diminished. In the past there was something of a folk art movement in southern Arizona making furniture and accessories from cactus wood.

Cardon *(Pachycereus pringlei)* is similar to saguaro but much larger. In fact, cardon is the largest of the cacti, growing to more than 60 feet at maturity and bearing many more stems than a saguaro. Young cardons have a bluish caste to the skin that becomes much greener at maturity. It can be hard to tell the difference between cardons and saguaros when young, but the spines of a saguaro are straight and dark, while those of a cardon are tan. Cardon flowers are held around the top of the stem and are a creamy white. But the fruit is unmistakable; it looks fuzzy from the ground but is covered with dense, golden spines.

I like the name **organ pipe cactus** *(Stenocereus thurberi)*. It sounds grand and full and imposing, so like the plant. Organ pipe cactus has numerous stems arising from a single base. The deep green of the skin is accented by short red-brown spines up the stems. This is a slow-growing cactus but well worth the wait. Give the plant plenty of room in a garden, as it will be more than 6 feet wide at maturity. The bloom is amazingly discrete: tiny pinkish blooms that appear up and down the ribs in summer. The tiny black fruit that follows is delicious to birds.

Senita *(Lophocereus schottii)*, along with organ pipe cactus, encroaches into Arizona only along the border with Mexico. Like organ pipe cactus, this species grows numerous stems from a single base. There is a lot of variation in individual senitas in the girth of the stem; some are barely the size of a woman's arm, while others are over 5 inches in width. Senita has a light blush on its green skin, giving it a dusky appearance. The spines are short and dark, spread far apart on the ribs.

There is an unusual variant form of senita known as **totem pole cactus** *(Lophocereus schottii* var. *monstrosa)*, which is from a limited area in the Baja. It is entirely without spines, and instead of the regular arrangement of ribs so routine in columnar cacti, it has a random array of rib sections and warty growths on the skin. All in all, it looks like a column of melted wax. Occasionally in very old age a stem will revert to a more normal form and show regular ribs and even bloom, although no fruit or seeds are set. There are two forms of this variant, one that is very large, with fat stems, and one that is much finer, with stems rarely more than 3 inches in diameter.

Mexican fence post *(Stenocereus marginatus)* is the most stunning of the columnar cactus in general cultivation. The multiple stems that arise from the base are deep, rich green. The ribs are outlined by a bright white, feltlike coating that provides an arresting contrast. The spines are short and spaced widely on the ribs. This species is frost sensitive, so it is wise to cover the tips when temperatures are expected to dip below freezing.

Old man of Mexico *(Cephalocereus senilis)* is most commonly seen as a potted plant. This species does well in the ground, however, if given some shade and well-drained soil. In a congenial site, it grows quickly to over 8 feet tall. The plant is multistemmed, but there are rarely more than five or six stems. Its most charming feature is the long white bristles that envelop the stems.

Hedgehog cacti, although small, are columnar cacti as well. This is a large group, most in the genus *Echinocereus*, and they are some of the most spectacular blooming plants for a desert garden. Grow this group with outstanding drainage, full sun, and minimal water for the best results.

The species most commonly called **hedgehog cactus** is *Echinocereus engelmannii*, which is frequently seen both in cultivation and in the hills of central and southern Arizona. The spines are long and dense on the plant, and there are usually a dozen or more stems. In April the plant explodes with a profusion of deep magenta flowers, so brilliant they can be seen for hundreds of yards in the desert. This can be a frustrating cactus to grow in some gardens. A bewildering combination of fungal and subsequent insect infestations can arise quickly, usually in warm weather, and literally eat out the heart of the plant.

There are many other beautiful species and varieties of hedgehog cacti, including *Echinocereus engelmannii* var. *bonkeri*, which has deep purple flowers and short spines; var. *nicholii*, remarkable for its large golden spines; the irresistible *Echinocereus triglochidiatus*, which has rose-red blooms and hundreds of stems; and the extremely cold-hardy *Echinocereus coccineus*, which bears scarlet flowers on short, tightly held stems.

Cleistocactus is a genus of columnar cacti that reminds me of an inquisitive snake. The plant's golden-spined stem runs along the ground for a foot or so, rooting as it goes, then unexpectedly rises straight up, often over 3 feet. If it encounters a creosote branch or another stem, it begins to fall over it, crawl under it, and then rise up again after a while. At the end of each of these wandering stems, flowers appear off and on throughout the summer. Tubular and generally closed (that is the meaning of *cleisto*), the flowers are red-orange with a chartreuse tip. This is an effortless plant to grow for such a charming addition to the garden.

One of the more common columnar cacti in desert gardens is the **night-blooming cereus** *(Cereus hildmannianus,* formerly *Cereus peruvianus).* Well-grown plants have dozens of stems over 5 feet tall arising from a common base. This cactus is tolerant of almost all soils, all watering regimes, and any light. It grows most beautifully and blooms best with at least a half day of sun and watering two or three times a month in the summer. The blooms are huge, trumpet-shaped white flowers that open at night all through the summer months. The blooms are followed by apple-sized red fruit that birds find irresistible.

Barrel Cacti

It began innocently enough. There were two or three small **golden barrel cacti** *(Echinocactus grusonii)* on the property when we bought the house. Rather than have them scattered around, we decided to plant them together under a creosote so that the long arms of the creosote would shelter them from the ferocious afternoon sun. Not long after, a friend gave us one that wasn't thriving in her kitchen, then a couple more arrived with some wonderful pots we bought. Now as I look out the kitchen window, I can see a colony of these flamboyant barrel cacti huddled at the base of the creosote. I like this species planted in groups; it focuses your eye on their magnificent intensity.

Golden barrels are moderately slow growing but will eventually be 3 feet tall and almost as wide. The top flattens somewhat, revealing a dense swirl of ribs, spines, and the feltlike covering of the growing tip. This is where the light yellow flowers appear in the summer. The flowers are not very showy, resembling dried straw flowers. Plants do best in partial shade overall, although I have seen many adjust to full sun if planted in the fall and planted very small. Plants grown in deep shade have pale, uninteresting spines.

Long known as **Easter lily cactus** *(Echinopsis x),* this small barrel cactus is a great favorite when it is in bloom but otherwise looks unremarkable. Most have deep green skin and very small spines. Some grow more than 8 inches tall, while others barely achieve 2 inches. All bloom with immense, trumpet-shaped flowers in the summer in a blinding array of colors. They are night blooming but will remain open until the sun hits them. These are an excellent choice for dry shade and do not do well in the full sun of the low desert.

The native barrels of Arizona are rugged, cold-hardy plants well suited to the rigors of growing without supplemental irrigation or the ministrations of a gardener. **Fishhook barrel** *(Ferocactus wislizenii)* and **compass barrel** *(Ferocactus* *cylandraceus)* are both taller than they are wide, usually 3 to 4 feet tall and about 12 inches in diameter. There are notable exceptions, both in nature and in gardens. These plants, like almost all members of the genus, require exceptional drainage and unadulterated full sun. Too much water or too little sun, and the plants begin to rot insidiously from within until one day they simply fall over, exposing a mushy interior. Both of these barrel cacti bloom in the dead middle of the summer, in July or August. Large yellow or orange flowers appear at the top of the plant and last for many days.

There are many other species of *Ferocactus*, some of which are outstanding. The **fire barrel** *(Ferocactus gracilis)* has remarkable fiery red spines. These plants are exquisite in the late winter light, appearing to glow from within. Be sure to put one where it will be backlit. *Ferocactus latispinus* has odd flattened spines that look like a fingernail. It has the unusual habit of blooming in the winter with a dark lavender flower.

The breadth of the genus *Mammillaria* is mind-boggling. There are hundreds of species, but they are generally of two forms: tiny, barrel-shaped plants that may be solitary or grow in great clusters, or tiny, columnar-shaped plants that always grow in large clusters. All of them bloom in delicate colors—pinks, rosy reds, and white—in late spring, holding their flowers around the top of the stem. All species make delightful additions alongside a rock or in a container. Plant them at close range so you can easily enjoy their tiny, fine spines and endearing flowers. A similar genus, *Coryphantha*, is nearly as large and as diverse, but generally the flowers are larger, more showy, and often darker in color.

Cacti with Jointed Stems

At first glance it is hard to imagine why prickly pears and chollas are in the same genus, *Opuntia*. The only thing they share is the habit of having jointed stems, which when flattened create the distinctive pads of prickly pears and when cylindrical create the branched form of chollas. Actually, their association is about to change. In the near future botanists will propose that this vast group be broken up into 15 different genera, hardly encouraging when I consider learning all those new names, but much more sensible, I am sure.

Both of these members of the genus *Opuntia* are easy to grow and very drought tolerant; most species are also quite cold hardy. They can be planted in the sunniest, hottest part of the garden, as long as they have good drainage, and will reward you with some of the showiest flowers found among desert flora. Opuntias generally have a slow to moderate growth rate but can easily be propagated. Just cut off a pad or joint, let it dry out for about a week, then stick it in the ground; water every couple of weeks to encourage rooting.

The plants we call cholla are a vast group of multistemmed, shrublike cacti. Many are very difficult to tell from one another, particularly without the flowers, but some are showy, effective garden plants. All are brutally armed and therefore should never be placed near a walkway, pool, or other high-traffic area. In most species the spines are barbed, making them difficult and painful to remove from your skin. So while this is my favorite group of cacti and I love to use them in the garden, I advise you to know what you are in for.

Staghorn cholla *(Opuntia versicolor)* is a highly variable plant that grows like a small shrub. The color of its flowers ranges from a pale yellow to a stunning magenta. **Buckhorn cholla** *(Opuntia acanthocarpa)* is similar in shape and, like staghorn cholla, is rarely over 5 feet tall. The flowers of buckhorn cholla are an odd yellow-green color that sometimes appears light brown or tan. **Tree cholla** *(Opuntia imbricata)* is a magnificent large shrub, usually over 6 feet tall and as wide, that is studded with deep purple blooms in late spring. The exquisite **silver cholla** *(Opuntia echinocarpa)* has a pale white sheath on the spines that turns the entire plant into a shimmering silver bush. **Cane cholla** *(Opuntia spinosior)*, perhaps the most attractive of the large shrubby chollas, has thick stems and bears dark lavender, red, or yellow flowers in the late spring. The fruit is bright yellow and hangs onto the plant in chains at least through the winter, sometimes longer.

The champion for fruit retention, however, is the **chain fruit cholla** *(Opuntia fulgida)*, often known quite erroneously as jumping cholla. This small-spined cactus is large; old plants exceed 15 feet in height. Every year the fruit is formed at the end of a long, pendulous chain that hangs from the end of a stem. The next year's fruit is set at the end of the chain, and after a number of years the chain can be nearly a foot long.

I believe the most beautiful cholla is **teddy bear cholla** *(Opuntia bigelovii)*, which has light yellow spines that turn the plant into a golden torch in the right light. This species is always numerous in nature; entire hillsides can be covered with it. While some plants bloom, they rarely set fruit; most of this cholla's increase is by the loss of little stems that then take root. This probably explains why there are such huge colonies of teddy bear cholla when it appears at all. This is a difficult plant to handle, but once it is in place, leave it alone, giving it enough room to form a small colony so you can enjoy the beauty of its glowing spines in your garden.

Two other chollas worth mentioning are Christmas cholla and pencil cholla. **Christmas cholla** *(Opuntia leptocaulis)* grows as a large group of very thin stems, generally under a tree or shrub. In fact, it is so easy to miss that you usually find it because you reached into the bush for something else and were caught by its spines. The stems are barely the size of a pencil, and the clear yellow flowers of summer are easy to miss. But the countless brilliant red fruits are held on the plant throughout the fall and winter; hence, the plant's name. Some Christmas chollas have large, golden spines; others are less showy; but all are worth growing both for their beauty and for the wildlife food they create.

Pencil cholla *(Opuntia aciculata)* grows countless stems about the size of a child's finger and is covered with widely spaced, long tan spines. Old plants can have a noticeable main stem, and some individuals are so regularly branched they look like a clipped bush. The skin is gray-green and blends well behind colorful perennials or with other succulents. The flowers are an unremarkable pale yellow and the fruit is green. It is the shape and form of the plant that makes it interesting in a garden.

Prickly pears have been garden and food plants for a very long time, particularly in Mexico. The great **Indian fig prickly pear** *(Opuntia ficus-indica)* may be a hybrid selection that was in use as a food plant in the Caribbean when Columbus arrived. It has a lot of a congenial agricultural habits: it is virtually spineless, the fruit is large and juicy, and the new pads are large and tender. This plant likes water, particularly during the hot summers of the lower desert. With well-drained soil, it can be watered every 10 to 14 days in the summer. This and the night-blooming cereus are among the few cacti that can tolerate growing along the berm of a flood-irrigated yard (common in the Phoenix area).

Many prickly pears look similar: low-growing plants with green skin, yellow or brown spines, and yellow flowers. These are generally **Engelmann's prickly pear** *(Opuntia engelmannii)* or **desert prickly pear** *(Opuntia phaecantha)*. Both species are a good choice for poorly irrigated areas or along the edges of a property where constant care is difficult.

For a little more pizzazz, try **chenille prickly pear** *(Opuntia acicularis)*. All prickly pears have short, fine bristles called glochids. They are usually so small that they are virtually invisible. The glochids of chenille prickly pear, however, are large and crowd the edge of the pad and each of the spines. The contrast of these dark orange-brown glochids and the yellow-green skin makes the plant interesting year-round. In the spring the cactus bears flowers in a stunning dark red-orange, making it even more attractive.

Most of us find it hard to resist the allure of the purple prickly pear *(Opuntia violaceae,* also known as *Opuntia santa-rita)*. The skin is a dusky blue-gray with various amounts of purple along the edge or around the spines. The color may intensify in cold weather or when the plant is under duress. In some individuals the color is persistent—they are purple all the time. In late spring the plant erupts with pure yellow flowers, forming a bush of incomparable splendor. Despite all its beauty, what I like best about purple prickly pear is its strong tendency to grow into a tight, shrubby form. Plants are generally 4 to 5 feet tall and as wide.

One more prickly pear to consider is the enchanting **beaver-tail** prickly pear *(Opuntia basilaris)*. This is a small prickly pear, rarely over 18 inches tall and 2 feet wide, with few pads. The skin is a dark blue-gray, dusky and deep, and the spines indent into the skin, making it look quilted. The flowers, a breathtaking shade of fuchsia, emerge much earlier than most prickly pear flowers, in late February or early March in Phoenix. This plant loathes water and is best grown under the most minimal irrigation plan. It is particularly resistant to summer watering, undoubtedly because of its Mohave Desert origins.

Vining Cacti

In southern Arizona on a June night, savvy desert gardeners begin to look for signs of bloom on the **Arizona queen of the night** *(Peniocereus greggii)*. This odd-looking plant is found in the southern Sonoran Desert at the base of creosotes and palo verdes, winding its way through their branches, perfectly camouflaged by its matching stems. The pitiful-looking gray stems are outlined with tiny black spines and arise from an immense swollen root. On one evening in June, the plant metamorphoses completely. Sometimes a few and often dozens of 8-inch tubular white blooms open in a long line along the stems, releasing their intoxicating, cloying smell into the desert. The entire show lasts one night, and usually all plants in one area bloom at one time.

Other vining cacti that are also night bloomers include *Harrisia bonplandii* and *Harrisia martinii*. Easy and effortless growers, they can be placed at the base of a mesquite or left to fall onto themselves. They do much better in some shade. Because they have formidable spines along the vine, they make a good choice if you have a low window or entry you would like to protect from intruders. *Acanthocereus pentagonus* is a large, dark green plant that will ramble and wander over a trellis or wall. Although very frost tender, it does well with the overhead protection of a tree or porch. Huge white flowers occur on the plant throughout the summer. This plant demands protection from the afternoon sun in the low desert. For the more adventurous gardener, plants such as **rattail cactus** *(Aporocactus* sp.*)* and members of the genus *Selenicereus* are tropical vining cacti. Rattail cactus has shocking magenta blooms in the spring, and the *Selenicereus* species bloom white.

Surely the oddest of all the vining cacti is *Pereskiopsis* sp. This plant is armed with both long spines and glochids but is unusual for also having true leaves. Luscious, satiny yellow flowers bloom in early summer and are followed by persistent bright yellow fruit that is shaped like a cigarette.

While sending a cactus up a trellis might sound absurd at first, consider that many vining genera are vines at home. The first trellis I built for my pereskiopsis was a large piece of pruned creosote branch, and it looked terrifically desertlike. Pereskiopsis is a fast grower, and soon my trellis was covered with its spiny, leafy stems packed with bright, translucent yellow flowers, then bedecked with curious elongated yellow fruit all summer. It became murderous to handle, and I was forced to add a redwood fan trellis. This trellis, too, is being overtaken, and soon a taller one will be required. I wish I had better anticipated the rampant growth in the beginning and thus avoided such a mishmash of trellises.

9 Agaves

I can honestly say that I never gave agaves a thought until I moved to Arizona. I am sure I knew they existed and had even seen a few as oddities, but I never paid any attention to them. I was living on the Gulf Coast, where there was usually a token agave or two around, but they were ill-suited to the muck and rain of that region.

After I arrived in Arizona, I still did not develop an interest in agaves immediately. In fact, I was not much impressed with them, and looking at the extensive collection at the Desert Botanical Garden was not much help. To me they all looked alike, too big and too dangerous. Finally I succumbed to a tiny plant in a 4-inch pot. I put it in the ground and watched it grow. That was the end of innocence and the beginning of passion.

That plant was a cow horn agave *(Agave bovicornuta)*, and it quickly grew into a masterpiece. The dark green leaves of this species are shiny, rounding out as they grow and pinch abruptly to a terminal spine. The spine and teeth on the leaf margins are maroon, typical of the fine color contrast so characteristic of agaves. Mine was a stunning plant, and by the time it bloomed after five years in the ground, I was a confirmed apostle of the agave. The delight I got from that plant induced me to look around. What I have found is a treasure trove of garden plants that are pitifully represented in desert gardening.

Most writers of gardening prose, sublime and mundane, have glossed over agaves. Henry Mitchell, who was a principal in the plant-right-to-life school, admitted to owning his first agave because he found it in a trash heap. He then described agaves as "dumb fiercely armed pets," and he liked them.

Others have been less kind. Most writers who spend a few words on agaves describe them as bizarre or vicious and advise the reader to be sure to give them plenty of room and keep children and pets at a distance, thus according agaves the status of garden pariah. Others describe the plants as being of wagon-wheel girth or cruelly thorny or mostly so gigantic that they are hardly worth space in your garden.

Recent authors of books on desert plants are more likely to suggest agaves to gardeners in the desert because they are useful or important. Such limp approval reminds me of trying to comfort a clumsy teen with the consolation that some people are late bloomers. These are pale words for such incredible plants and do not convey the interest and variation that such a large genus can offer a garden. There truly is an agave for every taste and every situation; their use is limited only by our imagination as gardeners.

Horticultural History...

The diversity of agaves is not well known to most gardeners, despite the wide distribution of the genus in the Americas. Agaves occur naturally from Utah to Honduras, growing in a variety of conditions, from rock outcrops and desert valleys to tropical forests and the higher slopes of snow-covered mountains. In addition, agaves display an impressive variety of size and form. They are most numerous in Mexico, adding to the incalculable number of ornamental plants available from that country. Of the 250 known species of agave, about 70 are cultivated.

Certain agaves have been in horticulture a long time. Spanish explorers noticed the plant immediately and took samples back to Spain. Many of these species found their way into private collections and botanical gardens in Europe. Linnaeus himself described the genus in 1753, creating the word *agave* from the Greek word *agauos*, which means noble or admirable.

The plants became valued curiosities. Many collections were maintained through the nineteenth century and into our own. Although most northern European collectors kept their plants as potted specimens, in Italy there was enough sun, warmth, and drainage to plant them out. Old gardens in Italy today, in particular La Mortola, still feature at least *Agave americana, Agave angustifolia,* and *Agave attenuata* in their collections.

It was from horticultural specimens in German, Dutch, English, and Italian collections that nineteenth-century botanists began serious descriptive work on the genus. To study them in their native Mexico required a long, difficult, and expensive journey. How much more congenial to spend time in the charming garden of a wealthy and generous collector, working out the taxonomy of these unusual oddities, than launching an expedition to an inhospitable, far-away place.

This approach presented a problem: plants grown in greenhouses in northern Europe or in too much shade no longer resembled themselves. Often they were pale; their leaves were elongated from low light; and they rarely bloomed, which created a misleading picture of the genus. In the early twentieth century, botanists began to seek out the species at home in the Americas. The work of Berger and Trelease and later H. S. Gentry opened the eyes of the botanical, and ultimately the horticultural, world to the astounding array of form, color, and size within the genus.

As botanists began to study the taxonomy of the genus, they realized that some species had been in cultivation so long that they could no longer be found wild. Gentry thought that he had located a wild member of *Agave americana*, but the origins of other cultivated species are more elusive. These observations imply that the species have been selected and modified through numerous generations of cultivation, revised by human intervention to the point that they are maintained only as horticultural specimens. Such species may actually have no truly wild members, or their wild counterparts may look so different that the relationship is masked.

This phenomenon is hardly unique to agaves. One need only look at the cereal grains and their wild analogues or at tomatoes, potatoes, corn, and a host of other useful plants to see that long, intensive cultivation has changed the plants dramatically. Outstanding ornamental agaves, such as *Agave desmettiana* and *Agave weberi*, appear to be horticultural clones from some long-lost ancestor kept in cultivation vegetatively because of their economic value, agricultural uses, and ease of culture. The same may be true of *Agave murpheyi*, *Agave americana*, *Agave fourcroydes*, *Agave sisalana*, *Agave tequilana*, and *Agave angustifolia*.

Uses of Agaves...

When the Spanish arrived, agaves were already in cultivation in many parts of the Caribbean and Mexico. The Spanish explorers found a number of the larger species—*Agave americana*, *Agave fourcroydes*, *Agave angustifolia*, *Agave sisalana*, and probably others—being grown for fiber and food. Agaves were planted in gardens, collected from the wild, and traded over great distances to keep valued clones alive.

The fiber was used then (as it still is today) throughout Mexico and Central America to make ropes, baskets, mats, hammocks, hats, and clothing. Agave rope is unrivaled for its combination of strength and flexibility.

Some time ago a visitor to the Desert Botanical Garden wrote me of his frustration in attempting to find the origin of a rope he had used as a young lariat thrower. He knew this rope as a maguey lariat. On his visit no one could tell him what a maguey plant was. It was my great pleasure to write him that *maguey* is a general term for *agave*, most often used in central Mexico, and that his lariat had come from these plants. He had remembered that lariat for more than 40 years when he wrote me a detailed description of it and the loops he had coaxed from it. It must have been an outstanding rope.

Historically, agaves in the desert regions of northern Mexico and the southern United States were eaten regularly. Just before the plant blooms, the leaves

Agave parryi *var.* truncata **MARY IRISH**

are removed from the bud and the large remaining bundle is roasted, usually in an open pit, then eaten. The bud at the brink of blooming is crammed with carbohydrates, which turn to sugars with the roasting, and the result is both nutritious and satisfying.

The Aztecs introduced the Spanish to pulque, an intoxicating fermented drink made from agave juice. There is evidence that the Aztecs learned of the drink from the people who lived in the highlands before their arrival. Haughty Aztec rulers declared the drink, or more probably its effect, to be a religious experience, and its use was reserved for priests and others of high orders. During a single festival they permitted the drinking of pulque, but drunkenness was tightly controlled. Punishments were prompt and severe.

Europeans brought the distillation process to Mexico, and now the production of distilled agave sap has become a viable industry in some regions. Tequila is the name of a distilled agave liquor made from clones of *Agave tequilana*, which are grown exclusively near the town of Tequila, in Oaxaca. All other distilled agave liquor is called mescal. The introduction of the worm to bottles of mescal is a recent marketing ploy that adds no significance or flavor to the drink.

Agaves in the Garden...

It is difficult to be neutral about agaves. Unlike trees or shrubs, agaves do not disappear in a confused planting. They are rarely subtle and make inferior backdrops, and once in bloom they are like spoiled children in their screams for attention. But what other ornamentals can offer such a combination of graceful form, resistance to tough growing conditions, and splendid variation? Desert gardeners are fortunate to have these species in the repertoire but are strangely reluctant to use them.

Container Plantings

One of the oldest fashions in growing agaves is to plant them in containers. Done out of necessity in parts of Europe, this remains a style that shows off the best features of the plants. The container itself can become an abundant miniature garden. Agaves in containers can establish a commanding frame for an entry or walkway or leap forward as an arresting eye stopper at a corner or down a long view. Gently armed or compact agaves make excellent accents around a pool.

There is no need to restrict potted agaves to those that work best in shade. A good number of dramatic agaves can thrive in the West's full sun. *Agave angustifolia*, especially its white variegated form, is a long-standing favorite for potted agaves. The striking *Agave victoriae-reginae,* with its crisp shape and near perfect symmetry emphasizing the dark green leaves lined with white, is a striking choice. If you have the place or the interest, this agave is best viewed from above, which allows both the symmetry and the coloring to be fully appreciated. *Agave ocahui,* with its dark green leaves trimmed in brown, *Agave parryi* var. *truncata,* and *Agave potatorum* are all extremely symmetrical agaves and make excellent choices for containers in the full sun.

Agaves do not have to grow alone in a pot. A container of agaves mixed with blooming plants can be particularly effective. Smaller lantana varieties, verbenas, or low-growing wildflowers such as nemophila or Mexican primrose make excellent companions for container-grown agaves.

Agaves for the most part tolerate container culture well, with a few special requirements. The root system of agaves, like that of most succulents, is not deep but is extensive in width. The roots are fibrous and radiate out from the plant like a wheel. In the ground this is a valuable adaptation to erratic and short-lived rainfall. In containers it means that ample room must be provided for the roots. The best pots for agaves are wider than they are deep. When choosing the size, remember that the more plant there is, the more root there is. Large agaves, such as *Agave vilmoriniana* or *Agave angustifolia,* need quite large pots, up to 36 inches in diameter, whereas the more diminutive *Agave toumeyana* ssp. *bella* or *Agave parviflora* will grow happily in pots 6 to 8 inches in diameter.

I have found agaves to be unfussy about soil in a container as long as it drains extremely well and is not mucky. A ratio of one part organic matter to five parts inorganic matter makes a good container soil, and even higher inorganic content works as well. Mix potting soil with fine gravel, aquarium gravel, pumice if you can find it, or sharp sand. It is generally a good practice to water agaves only when at least half the soil in the pot is dry in warm weather, and when it is dry nearly to the bottom in the winter. The plants grow mainly in the late spring and summer, so cool-weather watering need only be enough to prevent stress.

Container-grown agaves welcome fertilization on a monthly basis during the growing season. I use fish emulsion, but friends use a wide variety of fertilizers, soluble and not, all with excellent results. Commercial growers use fertilizers much more frequently and with much greater concentration; this treatment makes the plants look soft and luxuriant, but they are healthy and in excellent condition.

Agaves in containers can contract root mealy bug, especially in the summer. I suspect that too much organic matter in the mix and too frequent watering contribute greatly to these pests. Root mealy bugs must be treated quickly when they are found, for they multiply like rabbits. A strong solution of insecticidal soap will help keep them down, but you must apply it unfailingly twice a week. If the infestation is severe or persistent despite your efforts, the only truly effective treatment is to remove the plant from the pot, destroy the soil and the pot (unless it is precious, in which case you can thoroughly disinfect it), shake off as much soil as possible, and then soak the plant for 10 minutes in an insecticidal soap solution. Let the plant dry for a week, then repot it in fresh soil. This treatment is tedious if you are dealing with hundreds of small agaves, but it works.

Plantings in the Ground

It is in the ground that agaves come into their own as garden plants. In most of the arid West, agaves are well suited to the native, usually alkaline soils and require little or no soil amendment. A little compost or mulch added to the backfill of the planting hole is adequate. Resist using soil amendments for more than 25 percent of the volume of the backfill.

Planting itself is quite easy. Prevent future problems by allowing the roots to dry out for about a week before planting. Make sure the plant stays dry and rests in the shade during this time. Actually, agaves are very tough, and bareroot plants can be left for weeks out of the soil, a very helpful trait that agaves share with cacti and other succulents. Woody or herbaceous species just will not wait, but agaves will, and for this I am grateful. The plants will dry out and may wither, but recovery is simply a matter of planting, watering, and a little patience.

Because agaves have wide but not deep root systems, it is important that the planting hole be twice as wide as the plant and no deeper than the container from which it came. Spread the roots gently, using your hands to untangle them carefully. Allow the middle of the hole to be slightly higher than the sides, which helps reduce the risk of the crown sinking into the hole after the soil has settled and compacted. If too much water stands around it, the crown or growing point is susceptible to rotting, so it is wise to raise it slightly when planting.

As with most plantings in the low desert, it is advisable to put a small, shallow well around the plant. This serves two purposes: it prevents water from running away from the plant, and it permits water to percolate slowly into the soil. Sizing a basin is not an exact task. In general, if the basin extends beyond the plant by about half of its diameter, that is enough. The basin will need to be increased as the plant matures.

Newly planted agaves need to be watered thoroughly. After that, the watering schedule depends upon the time of the year. Fall is the best time to plant almost anything, including agaves, in the low desert. Agaves planted in fall need to be watered twice a week during the first month and then every one to two weeks as the weather cools. Established agaves often need no supplemental watering in the winter if there are rains every month; otherwise, a good soak once a month will suffice.

It is important to water agaves sufficiently during warm weather; this means about every week in the summer, especially when it is hot and dry. This does not mean walking by them with a hose in your hand but, rather, giving them a deep, slow soaking that will replenish the soil moisture. A rainfall, of course, replaces the need to water. Agaves can be watered quite a lot, as long as the soil is rocky and has very open drainage. Plants that wilt and have shriveled or yellowing leaves are usually plants that are not being watered enough, regardless of the time of year. Do not be afraid to look at your plants to determine if they need water; automated timers are very poor gardeners.

Many agaves have pale or yellowed leaves in the low desert when the temperatures are high, over 108°F. If these plants are kept well watered and shaded a little if possible, the damage is temporary, and leaf color will be restored when the temperatures cool.

Agaves are often sold in this area in small pots, and these plants are a great buy. Planted out in a satisfactory place, the plants grow quickly and become beautiful in a few years. The patience to begin with small plants and allow them to mature in your garden is an acquired talent. Gardens are places not only of care, cultivation, and beauty; they are weavings where the slow unfolding of innumerable intertwined lives emerges gracefully. Most agaves require a number of years to mature, from 7 years in smaller species to as much as 40 in large ones. In the same way in which you would give a plant adequate space, give it the time to grow and blend with the rest of the garden and for you to become familiar with its ways.

Mixed Plantings

One of the finest uses for any agave is as a contrast with other perennial plantings. Soft billowing shapes can become boring, even if they do bloom beautifully, and the sharp, hard edges of an agave rosette set them off perfectly, providing outstanding visual relief. Considering that agaves come in combinations of green and maroon *(Agave bovicornuta)*, blue-gray *(Agave colorata, Agave weberi, Agave parryi,* and *Agave potatorum)*, dark green with white accents and bristles *(Agave victoriae-reginae, Agave filifera, Agave schidig-*

era, Agave filifera, Agave parviflora, and *Agave toumeyana),* dark green
(Agave scabra and *Agave angustifolia),* or light green *(Agave bracteosa, Agave
desmettiana,* and *Agave attenuata),* there should be a color suitable for any
perennial planting.

Wildflower plantings also benefit from an inclusion of the dark, erect shape
of agaves. The contrast of these sword-shaped succulents with the softness of
penstemon, lupine, desert marigold, or bladderpod makes a marvelous mixed
planting.

For a long time I imagined that agaves would make a stunning allee. At last
I found one in central Phoenix, and it is everything I thought it could be. It is
in an older neighborhood with lots of citrus on the property. The house sits far
back from a busy street. The long, straight driveway is lined with a double row
of plants, tall desert fan palms in the back and *Agave sisalana* in front, the
entire planting backed by the dense green citrus. It resembles an honor guard,
and whenever the agaves bloom out, it is going to be spectacular.

Blooming...

The melodramatic approach of most agaves to blooming, that is, just once in
their lifetime, accounts for much of the reluctance to using them in the garden. Why invest such a lot of time and energy in a plant that is going to die
once it blooms? is a question I am often asked. To me this is a shortsighted
approach to the plants. I do not find it so different from using annuals, which
are stunning in their display that lasts for only a few weeks, at which time the
plants suddenly expire. I do not hear much talk about giving up growing annuals, despite their one-year life span.

The blooming of an agave is an event. It is cause for grabbing a chair, setting up an observation post, and enjoying the show. The stalk develops quickly,
sometimes growing as much as 12 to 14 inches per day. And it is big. Even in
small agaves the stalk is enormous compared to the plant. In *Agave toumeyana*
the plant is rarely over a foot tall, but the bloom stalk soars 8 feet. In larger
plants stalks can rise 40 feet in the air.

Agave stalks bear flowers in two basic styles: spicate, or closely attached,
looking like a torch of bloom, or paniculate, resembling a candelabra with the
flowers held in bunches at the ends of small branches. Usually the flowers are
yellow or gold, but there are grand exceptions. *Agave bracteosa* flowers are
white; *Agave pelona* flowers are wine red.

All of this hoopla takes place, of course, to be sure that the flowers get pollinated. Agaves are pollinated by a number of cooperative creatures, including

bees, moths, birds, and bats. The flowers of many agaves are hard and rigid, held out from the plant on sturdy branches. This adaptation allows bats, which are heavy, to feed and incidentally pollinate the flowers without destroying them. The plant reciprocates this arrangement by offering vast amounts of nectar to the insects, birds, and bats.

The agave fruit is a pod full of tightly packed black, flat, papery seed. Agaves are extremely easy to grow from seed and germinate best in warm weather. I use a 50/50 mix of perlite and vermiculite to prevent fungal infections and the need for fungicides. The germination of fresh seed is astounding, and even four-year-old seed will germinate within a week. As with most seed, it is wise to keep the seed refrigerated if you must store it. Young agave plants benefit from regular fertilization to grow steadily and continuously.

There can be a problem with growing agaves from the seed of your own plants. Agaves are promiscuous hybridizers. Their flowering style encourages and sometimes requires that the flowers not be self-pollinated. As birds, bats, and insects move from agave to agave with their bills, faces, and bodies full of pollen, they create hybrids. If you want the seed to be pure, you must pollinate it yourself or obtain seed from a reputable dealer.

Agave Snout Weevil...

The small agave snout weevil is particularly fond of using the bud of agaves as the nursery for its larvae. A female weevil tastes her way around the garden, looking for plants with a particular flavor or chemical signature. When she finds one, she lays her eggs. Agaves marshal all their carbohydrates for blooming, and it is this carbohydrate load that feeds the weevil larvae during their development. This problem is insidious; symptoms of agave snout weevil infestation are nearly invisible until the plant suddenly begins to collapse. The leaves spread and fall, leaving the bud standing like a spike. Soon it, too, collapses. At this point nothing can save the plant. It is for this reason that *Agave americana* is rarely seen to bloom.

Weevils can be treated to a great extent if you understand their life cycle. Young plants are rarely susceptible to the weevil, but as a plant gets older and near to blooming age, the weevil becomes more of a threat. Eggs and larvae can be killed with a judiciously timed application of Diazinon, a potent chemical that must be used carefully and exactly as described on the label. Watch for small holes in the leaves near the base, a sure sign of a female weevil entry. Spread the chemical liberally around the base of the plant and work it into the ground gently. Water it in thoroughly. While Diazinon has a fairly long life, it does not last the entire lifetime of an agave, and repeat dosages may be necessary.

Agave toumeyana *GARY IRISH*

It is important to remove an agave infested with the weevil and kill all the larvae you can find. There will be a lot of them, and as the plant is pulled out, they will be quite visible. It is unwise to replant the pups or bulbils of the mother plant, which has already demonstrated itself to be vulnerable to the weevil. If you can find offspring from a plant that has bloomed, it is quite likely they will be less susceptible to weevil damage.

I cannot personally adjust myself to the use of chemical treatments, and therefore I take the tactic of using agaves that are less susceptible to the weevil. In general, the large-leaved giants, such as *Agave americana, Agave angustifolia*, and *Agave chrysantha*, are more vulnerable to the weevil. The likelihood of attack is less in medium- to smaller-sized agaves and those with hard leaves.

The other no-chemical strategy is just to enjoy the plant during its lifetime in your garden. The weevil times her egg laying with blooming, and if left to bloom, your agave will die anyway.

Agave Choices...

Soft-Leaved Agaves

Agave vilmoriniana, known as **octopus agave**, is a striking plant with graceful arching leaves that turn and reach for the ground like a dancer bowing. In the ground this agave can be 4 to 5 feet tall and nearly 6 feet across. Although it will not grow so large in a container, it can still be used to create dramatic effect. I saw a most original planting idea for this agave at a garden show in Phoenix. Carrie Nimmer had designed a small garden generally planned as a courtyard devoted to desert plants of the world. As you entered this small courtyard, extremely colorful plants drew your eye along paths radiating out from a central point. But at this central point, where you would expect a fountain or a statue, she had placed a majestic *Agave vilmoriniana*. It was in effect an agave fountain, and it was magnificent. I am determined to have one when we develop that part of the yard we lovingly know as "the outback."

Octopus agave does well in full sun, even in containers, although light or partial shade from the western sun is advisable in the low desert. It is somewhat frost tender but needs protection only when temperatures are expected below 27°F. A light frost blanket is all that is needed to prevent any damage.

Agave desmettiana, an urn-shaped plant with celadon green leaves, does well in deep shade but looks best with a half day of sun. It is reported to be quite cold tender, but I have found it to be an excellent ornamental plant if it is given overhead protection. I have planted one under the branches of a palo brea, in deep shade, and it has withstood temperatures in the low twenties. Although it suffered some leaf damage, it recovered quickly and is still a fine specimen. Others in pots have survived 18°F in an unheated greenhouse.

The leaves of *Agave desmettiana* often show a disfiguring spotting in the winter due to the cold. The leaves become spotted, some with light spots, some with dark, and look generally unhealthy. The spots fade quickly when warm weather returns. The key to such tolerance is protection from frost. Whether the overhead protection is from a tree, a shrub, the eaves of a house, a blanketlike covering, or a greenhouse, such cover extends the cold tolerance of many plants dramatically.

Smooth-leaved agaves not only are excellent container plants but can create an exotic, tropical look for a patio or courtyard. One of the most widely used agaves for this purpose is *Agave attenuata*, the darling of numerous Mediterranean and southern California gardens. This unusual agave has a large rosette of unarmed wide, light green leaves arising from a whitish stem. The stem can become 3 feet tall, and the plant reaches, bends, and twists in peculiar and often gravity-defying ways. It is best grown in partial shade in the low desert and needs protection from the full sun. This species is quite cold tender, making overhead protection a must.

Agave guiengola, a species known to the scientific world for only 30 years, comes originally from a limestone formation in Oaxaca by the same name. The plant has extremely wide leaves that are pale gray-blue and rimmed with fine, dark, small teeth. Its few leaves give it a wide, flat look, and it is a spectacular specimen plant. Finding it may require looking, but this species is more than worth the trouble. It, too, grows best in light shade and with significant overhead protection from frost. Be prepared to cover it during a cold snap.

Agave bracteosa is excellent in the shade but can grow in great amounts of sun if you give it time to acclimate to it. This is one of the lesser-known agaves in horticulture, but that is the gardener's loss. The plant has fine, thin, curved leaves and grows only to 2 feet. Like many agaves, it makes a great number of root suckers, also known as pups. In a few years they become an agreeable clump of agaves. For the most part, agave plants die following bloom. *Agave bracteosa* is a pleasant exception, blooming throughout its lifetime. From all the accumulated root suckers, a forest of 4- to 6-foot-tall spikes with white flowers arises and lasts for weeks, guaranteed to light up any dark corner you have.

Large Agaves

Two large agaves, *Agave angustifolia* and *Agave americana*, have become excessively common in the warm, dry parts of the world. *Agave angustifolia* is a linear-leaved agave that is quite beautiful. One variety shows white striping on the leaves, and there is a yellow form as well. I confess that I have never met a yellow variegated plant that I liked, as I think they all look sickly, but the white variegated form of this agave is stunning. I have seen it alone as an outstanding point plant or as a touch of white in a frothy sea of green groundcover. It is beautiful either way. *Agave angustifolia* was one of the first agaves brought back by the European explorers and has long been in ornamental horticulture. It is also a valued fiber plant in many areas of Mexico and is grown today in support of that industry.

Without a doubt, it is the huge, overbearing gray giant *Agave americana* that is the first agave most gardeners recall. This, too, is a species long in Western horticulture and Mexican agriculture, but how it became the signature agave in gardens is beyond me. First of all, it is immense, over 6 feet tall, and needs a large space to look its best. Even more of a problem in low desert areas is that it is extremely susceptible to the devastation of the agave snout weevil.

Agave weberi has a delicate look despite being 4 to 5 feet tall and nearly as wide. The leaves are a light bluish gray, sometimes nearly white, and are almost spineless. In the full sun the plant has an open, graceful rosette. When grown in the shade, the leaves can become severely etiolated, elongating to nearly twice their normal size. This agave is more sensitive to light than most and will change its character significantly in either strong light or deep shade.

Other large species, such as *Agave gigantensis*, with its Bali dancer pose of graceful, curving leaves, and *Agave zebra*, which develops into a flattened thundercloud of a plant, are spectacular if given enough room to grow. Both become about 4 feet tall, spreading to the same dimension.

Agave geminiflora and *Agave stricta* have unusual leaves that are nearly round and so numerous the plants resemble a sea urchin. They are excellent foils for a perennial planting with too many leafy plants; their sharp, pointed leaves provide a welcome contrast.

Small to Medium-Sized Agaves

One of the easiest medium to small agaves to locate for a low desert garden is *Agave parryi*. This species is native to a large part of Arizona at high elevations in the center of the state. In the mountains on the Mexican border, you find *Agave parryi* var. *huachucensis*, and in Sonora the extraordinary *Agave parryi* var. *truncata*. They are all beautiful, tightly formed agaves that have gray-blue leaf edges with dark teeth and a dark terminal spine. *Agave parryi* is cold hardy in the low desert, but *Agave parryi* var. *truncata* may need protection in the coldest areas. This variety has much wider leaves than average, and the color contrast is more intense, making it one of the more ornamental agaves of its size.

Agave murpheyi has a fascinating association. It is thought to be a cultivated variety kept alive over the centuries as a food source. Its habit of making thousands of bulbils on a single stalk has undoubtedly extended its usefulness. In Arizona this species is found only in proximity to historical Native American sites, another clue to its historical cultivation. *Agave murpheyi* is quite ornamental as well. Although there is some variation, most are 3 to 4 feet tall and about as wide. The leaves are narrow, and the skin is a dark blue-gray. The terminal spine is short, as are the teeth on the leaves. This is a tough agave and will thrive in the full sun in Phoenix, demanding only that there be adequate drainage.

The stunning leaf imprints of *Agave colorata* are mesmerizing. Leaf imprints develop during the formation of the bud, when the leaves are squeezed tightly together, etching the impression of the well-armed leaf margins on the back of each layer of leaves. As the leaves open, the image becomes increasingly pronounced and remains intact throughout the life of the leaf. These light, almost white impressions on the gray-blue urn-shaped leaves set this medium-sized agave apart from most others.

Two agaves not in common usage, *Agave schidigera* and *Agave filifera*, are beautiful medium-sized plants. Both have dark green leaves vividly marked with white and feature flowing white filaments. These agaves look wonderful peeking out from a rocky border, as an accent in plantings under large trees, or as a feature plant in a raised planter.

Agave pelona, Agave ocahui, Agave scabra, Agave havardiana, and *Agave neomexicana,* all growing up to 4 feet tall, offer excellent gardening possibilities. The rosette of each is particularly symmetrical, and their leaf color combinations are quite striking. *Agave pelona* and *Agave ocahui* have linear dark green leaves without large teeth and are lined in a dark wine color or in white, respectively. *Agave scabra,* a deep intense green, is heavily armed with multifaceted teeth. *Agave havardiana* and *Agave neomexicana* have blue-gray, wide leaves that are exquisitely formed.

For difficult sites too hot or dry for most plants, choose *Agave deserti,* a medium-sized agave that is extremely drought tolerant. *Agave deserti* is a lovely plant with the blue-gray cast that works well with brightly colored perennials or wildflowers. *Agave lechuguilla,* a narrow-leaved green agave, is also admirably suited for the hottest, driest spot in the garden.

One of my favorite smaller agaves is *Agave macroacantha,* which has light blue-gray leaves accented by deep maroon leaf edges and terminal spine. This species grows well in light shade. In Phoenix it is quite hardy to the cold but needs protection in Tucson and higher elevations. It is a charming agave that forms a clump of about a dozen perfectly formed rosettes.

Small, even tiny hard-leaved agaves, such as *Agave toumeyana* ssp. *bella* or *Agave parviflora,* make interesting specimen plants, especially in containers. The leaves of these lovely pixies are perfectly formed into tight, regular rosettes, strikingly marked with white streaks, and further defined by fine white filaments floating off the leaves.

I often see *Agave toumeyana* ssp. *bella* emerging from a rocky slope, mixed with hedgehog cacti, dudleyas, a smattering of small grasses, and wildflowers. It is the most delightful natural garden scene I have found in Arizona, and yet it is not reproduced in gardens around the area. With its remarkable form and color, such a collection of small plants, hard rocks, pointed-leaf agaves, soft, bright dudleyas, and erect hedgehogs with brilliant magenta flowers would make a sensational container garden.

Aloe marlothii *GARY IRISH*

10 Other Succulents

Succulence is such an alien trait. Imagine being able to store all the water you would need for two, three, or four months. Commonly regarded as a characteristic of cacti, succulence in fact occurs throughout the plant world. There are succulent members of the grape, sunflower, lily, butterfly weed, and dogbane families, as well as the ice plant and crassula families, which are solely succulent. Mind-boggling in their diversity of form, a great many succulents are worthwhile and even desirable components of desert gardens.

Succulent Choices...

Aloe

Naturally, when it comes to succulents in the garden, one must begin with aloes. Many find it hard to tell an aloe from an agave. They share a certain similarity of form: long-lived leaves in a rosette pattern, often numerous offsets, and rough or thorny leaf edges.

Aloe flowers have petals, usually orange, red, or yellow, that have stamens tucked inside; the flowers are generally small and thin and are attached to the flowering stalk by a tiny stem. Agave flowers generally have fused petals (called tepals) that are yellow, gold, or reddish; stamens are held far outside the tepals. The flowers are sturdy, upright, and generally closely attached to the blooming stalk.

When the plants are not in bloom, look closely at the edge of leaves. In agaves the teeth derive from separate tissue, and by closely examining the edge, you can see a line of separation between leaf and tooth. Most agaves also have a sharp, hard, terminal spine at the end of each leaf. In aloes the teeth are a part of the leaf. They look like taffy that has been pulled up from the leaf and dried. Aloes rarely have a sharp, hard, terminal spine.

Most aloes do best with some shade, particularly in the summer, and infrequent summer irrigation. Like many succulents from Africa, they are winter growing and winter blooming here. Many aloes are frost tender and benefit from covering with a frost blanket or overhead protection from the bough of an evergreen tree.

Aloe vera (the common and scientific name) is so widespread as to be banal. Aloe vera may bloom either orange or yellow in great spikes of color throughout the late winter and earliest spring. The medicinal properties of this species are legendary, an attribute it shares with only three or four other members of the genus. The gelatinous sap from a leaf will relieve the pain and discomfort of burns, scrapes, minor abrasions, and other skin irritations.

Aloe vera, like most aloes, grows best in filtered sun. Plants grown in full sun will live and bloom, but they turn pale and become washed with red accents, which are a sure sign of stress in succulents.

Aloe vera is far from the only aloe that is useful in desert gardens. The tree-like or arborescent species, such as *Aloe marlothii, Aloe ferox, Aloe dichotoma,* and *Aloe ramosissima,* are fascinating additions to a garden. *Aloe marlothii* is quite cold hardy in the low desert and with overhead protection will remain undamaged to 25°F. The leaves of this species and *Aloe ferox* are difficult to tell apart because both are large and thick and have a variable number of warty spines on them. The flowers however, are quite different. The flowers of *Aloe marlothii* are yellow and arranged along one axis of the branching pedicels. In *Aloe ferox* the inflorescence is more erect, and the fiery red to red-orange flowers are found around the pedicel.

Aloe dichotoma is more difficult to grow here except in a pot but is so beautiful it is irresistible. This species is particularly sensitive to overwatering in warm months and to poor drainage. In favorable conditions, though, it grows quickly to 8 to 10 feet tall. While this may sound grand, remember they are 20 to 30 feet tall in nature.

Aloe ramosissima is a personal favorite. It produces its distinctive branching habit even at a young age. The flowers are a brilliant bright yellow, and there can be two to six inflorescences per plant. This species is much more cold hardy than previously thought, and in an area with good drainage it will be undamaged at temperatures around 25°F.

Perhaps one of the showiest of the tall aloes is *Aloe vaombe.* Throughout the summer its long, shiny leaves are a dark, rich green. With the coming of cold weather, they turn a vibrant deep red. This stunning red accent in the winter garden is wonderful when coupled with the spreading, branched, blooming head of scarlet flowers. Such seasonal brilliance is one of the most desirable aspects of growing aloes for winter gardens.

Another worthwhile aloe for the garden is actually a vine, *Aloe ciliaris.* Because the plant does not have tendrils or other clinging structures, it must be given a trellis, tree, or shrub in which to climb. I knew of one once that was the wonder of its neighborhood, growing on a dead pine stump. Delicate caps of clear red flowers occur in February and March, adding even more interest to the plant.

There are countless smaller aloes, from the minuscule *Aloe bakeri*, *Aloe descoginsii*, and *Aloe jucunda*, to the medium- and moderate-sized *Aloe gracilis* and *Aloe chabaudii*. Interplanted in perennial beds, these plants offer excellent contrast and relief from the monotony of perennials when they are out of bloom. Hummingbirds are strongly attracted to aloe blooms, adding yet another reason to grow them in large numbers in the garden.

Euphorbia

There are hundreds of succulent euphorbias, and because they have spines on the stem, they are often confused with cacti. There are three good ways to tell them apart: euphorbia spines are almost always a pair united at the base, while cacti thorns never are paired; euphorbias do not have areoles (those distinctive feltlike structures that are the hallmark of cacti), but all cacti have them; and the flowers of euphorbias are a complicated cuplike structure and quite small, while the flowers of cacti are large and showy.

I am not a great fan of succulent euphorbias, which all look too similar and too plain for my taste, and I say that with all due deference to their legions of fans. Two, however, do have a home in my garden: Moroccan mound and crown of thorns. **Moroccan mound** *(Euphorbia resinifera)* forms a dense, tight cluster of 6- to 8-inch stems in either full sun or partial shade. It is the most effortless of plants; occasional water in the summer is enough to keep it in good shape and to allow for steady growth. In May it blooms with tiny cups of yellow along the ribs of the stems.

Crown of thorns *(Euphorbia milii)* is a highly variable species. One variety with extremely large leaves becomes a shrub up to 5 feet tall and 6 feet in diameter. Its inflorescence is equally large, and the individual flowers are about half an inch long. Other varieties are no more than 8 inches tall, and the flowers are barely a quarter inch in size. Flower color in this species ranges from pink to cream to bicolor to, most commonly, red. Wonderful as a potted plant, crown of thorns also grows beautifully in the ground in partial shade if it has terrific drainage and moderate watering. In a pot it can easily accept watering once a week; in the ground twice a month in summer is adequate to keep it fully leafed out and blooming. Should it become drought stressed or dried out, the leaves will yellow and fall, but good watering will bring it back into leaf.

Somewhat frost tender, crown of thorns needs overhead protection during a bad freeze but will recover quickly from minor frost damage. The best thing about this species is that it blooms virtually year-round.

Sansevieria

Sansevieria is a genus that achieved great popularity in Victorian times as house plants and has endured since as sturdy, reliable potted plants. In the low desert sansevierias have great garden potential. Tough, immensely variable, and drought tolerant, they solve one of the most gnarly problems of desert gardening: dry shade. Best known of the group is **mother-in-law's tongue** (*Sansevieria trifasciata* and its numerous forms and cultivars). Equally of merit are the tall, elegant *Sansevieria cylindrica*, with its long, rounded stems that end in a sharp tip arranged like a fan; *Sansevieria aethiopica*, with its sturdy, short, nearly round leaves usually about 6 to 8 inches tall; *Sansevieria fasciata*, which has larger, flat leaves; *Sansevieria hahnii* and others that are often sold as **bird nest sansevieria;** and *Sansevieria stuckyi*, which has more or less linear leaves. All sansevieras do best in partial to deep shade in the low desert.

Soils are immaterial to most of them but should be well drained and free from ponding. Sansevierias spread by rhizome, similar to iris, and can be divided or reduced by cutting the rhizomes in the early fall. On a drip irrigation system they should be located far away from emitters because regular, steady water will rot them quickly.

Mesemb

When I started introducing new plants from the Desert Botanical Garden's collection, I was intrigued by mesembs, also known as ice plants. At that time most in the trade were brought in from California, and while they were imminently suitable for coastal conditions, they quickly withered and died in the low desert heat. Yet as I looked around, I found numerous species in many genera that looked good in our summers and thrived in our winters. Later the talented horticulturist Cathy Babcock began to plant some out in fuller sun to find out how they behaved. From these efforts began the introduction and sale of *Malephora crocea, Ruschia caroli, Lampranthus multiradiatus, Drosanthemum speciosum,* and others.

Malephora crocea is a lovely low-growing plant with fat, water-filled leaves nearly impervious to the sun and heat of the low desert. The leaves turn brown or rusty red in full sun, but the plant remains healthy and rewards the gardener with copper-colored flowers in winter.

Ruschia caroli is a finer, more delicate plant. Its leaves are barely a quarter inch wide and trail along the ground. The bloom is wonderful, a winter carpet of pale pastel pink. This species usually grows and blooms better in partial shade but will endure full sun in winter.

Lampranthus multiradiatus is a shrub usually less than 2.5 feet tall. Densely covered with flattened, succulent, gray-green leaves, it is handsome, making a fine addition to a dry perennial bed, a succulent garden, or even a perennial planting. The flowers cloak the plant in vivid pink through January and February. The effect is so stunning it will make you stop, stare, and wonder at such beauty from so homely a plant.

A species frequently labeled *Drosanthemum speciosum* but probably is not has deep, dark magenta flowers and small leaves. I have heard that the ones in the Phoenix area come from a planting found cascading over a wall in Globe, Arizona. Certainly there is a charming rock wall or two in Globe covered with this plant, but its exact origins in horticulture are more elusive. A great plant, it is hardy to the cold and resistant to all but the most intense reflected heat. Its only drawback is that the color is so commanding it is difficult to use with anything else. I like the plant best in containers, where it becomes a piece of brilliance, like a jewel, all on its own. I feel the same way about the real *Drosanthemum speciosum*, which blooms a scintillating bicolor yellow and orange that is nearly blinding. This species is variable and can bloom in many colors.

Cephalophyllum is a large genus of mainly ground-hugging succulents with extremely large, brilliant flowers. One that has been grown at the Desert Botanical Garden for a long time is of uncertain name but has brilliant purple flowers. The species *Cephalophyllum alstonii* is vibrant red. There are others that are white flowered and do well here, mainly in partial shade and with a drastic reduction in summer watering.

One of the botanical wonders of this family is the tiny annual *Dorotheanthus bellidiformis*. This species grows nearly flat on the ground, has succulent leaves, and explodes every afternoon with variously colored flowers, making it a veritable garden in its own right. The flower colors range from deep magenta to pink, white to purple, and often are multicolored. If you can find the seed, broadcast it in the fall, but plants can be transplanted at any time from October through January and will bloom that year.

Mesembs as a group are strongly summer dormant, and it is wise to leave them in a location where water can be carefully controlled during the summer. They can rot easily with too much water given too regularly during this time. These species also need soils fairly high in minerals, as well-amended soils are too waterlogged and tight for them to thrive.

For many of them the best culture is in pots—large, flat ones that show them to great advantage during the winter, when they are most splendid. Then, when it is time for their reduced watering and the summer doldrums, they can be moved to a shady dry spot and given only intermittent watering. In the winter when they are growing and blooming, they want full sun.

The choices in succulents for desert gardens hardly stop there. Succulent members of the genus *Oxalis*, known to many gardeners as a pernicious and obnoxious weed, make spectacular additions to small gardens and rock gardens. Haworthias and gasterias, in a smorgasbord of sizes, are quite congenial to culture outside, particularly in lots of summer shade. This is a group for experimentation but one that can provide both extended color and unique interest to any desert garden.

11 *Distinctive Desert Plants*

There are a number of highly ornamental species in desert gardens that defy ready characterization as a group. They are perennials, but because that term has a long association with herbaceous plants, it is misleading. Many are woody but do not really look like a shrub or a tree. Others are succulent or partially so, but because they are not fleshy in their leaves or stems, that term also can be misleading. A group name for these species is elusive, but there is no doubt that ocotillo, hesperaloe, yucca, desert spoon, beargrass, and their relatives have a natural fit in any desert garden.

Distinctive Choices...

Fouquieria

Ocotillo *(Fouquieria splendens)* is at the heart of every vista in the upper Sonoran Desert. Its long, sturdy canes rise high above the desert floor, topped with fiery red-orange flowers in spring and any time thereafter that it rains. Ocotillo occurs naturally in dense hillside forests, but in gardens more frequently appears as a solitary specimen. While an individual plant makes a stunning focal point or solo specimen, a garden of the scale to accept a forest or a long entry of ocotillo would be breathtaking.

The culture of ocotillo is easy in low desert regions, but elsewhere care must be taken to provide extremely good drainage, the hottest possible site, and minimal freezing temperatures. Ocotillo can be planted at any time, but early spring and fall are best. Despite its stunning drought tolerance when established or mature, ocotillo requires steady, regular watering to become established after transplanting. Water deeply two or three times per month during the entire first summer, using basins or wells to collect and hold water around the emerging root system.

Often gardeners are advised to spray ocotillos rather than water them. This is ridiculous. It is the roots that take up water and nutrients (the case in nearly all plants), and it is the roots that need the water. Transplanted ocotillos, particularly those that have suffered extensive root damage, often will require a year or longer before producing leaves after transplant. Check the stem; if the

Soaptree yucca (Yucca elata) **MARY IRISH**

stem shows any green and is pliable, the plant is alive and will recover with good care. If it snaps or is a dull gray, the cane is dead.

When buying a bare-root ocotillo, take a long, hard look at it. It should have pliable canes that show some green and should have as large a root system as possible. In addition, bare-root plants should have a tag demonstrating that they have been dug legally. Demand the tag; otherwise you may be supporting the illegal digging and transfer of these plants.

I find there is much variation between individual ocotillos. Some individuals are stiff and upright, while others have graceful drooping canes. Some plants retain their leaves nearly all the time, yet others grow leaves only as barely required, regardless of weather and water conditions. Flower color likewise is highly variable, ranging from a bright, brilliant red to a dull reddish orange, and there is even the odd yellow flower from time to time. What would be pretty, I think, is a white-flowered form, and although I have heard reports of this color form, I have yet to see it.

Two other species in the genus are irregularly found in desert gardens but could be used much more. **Tree ocotillo** *(Fouquieria macdougalii)* is native to Sonora and branches into a 4- to 6-foot shrub. Deep scarlet flowers are held at the tip of the branches in clusters, giving the effect of a red sparkler. **Palo adan** *(Fouquieria diguetii)* branches more densely than ocotillo from a short stem. Palo adan flowers range from a pale red-pink to deep red. Care and cultivation are the same as for ocotillo.

The bizarre **boojum** *(Fouquieria columnaris)* is a wonderful curiosity in the garden, with its pale trunk that narrows toward the top and radial spiny stems that cover the entire column. This can be a challenging and difficult plant to fit into an overall design. A lush planting of creosote around it and smaller agaves and other succulents at its feet would help to bring it into focus.

Boojums are surprisingly delicate. It is extremely important not to break the skin while moving them, because such injuries can introduce bacteria and other infections. In the ground boojums grow quickly with sufficient winter water, and in fact, reports of individuals that have grown 10 to 11 feet in five years are not uncommon. Sadly, such plants are usually inadvertently planted in the path of a roof drain or other water-harvesting device, and one wet season, particularly a wet winter, will finish it off. Watering one or two times per month in the winter promotes a steady, healthy growth of stems. Less water results in fewer stems and a spare, gangly look. In any event, make sure that water does not pond or hold around a boojum.

Boojums are summer dormant; their leaves begin to yellow and drop off in early April. Do not mistake this as a sign the plant needs more water, but let it go dormant and rest during the summer. Sometime in the fall, usually by the first of November, leaves will reemerge and the entire cycle will begin again. Oddly enough, boojums bloom in the middle of summer, when they are entirely dormant, but the cream-colored flowers, although curious and interesting, are not especially ornamental.

Hesperaloe

Red hesperaloe *(Hesperaloe parviflora)*, sometimes known as red yucca, is an indestructible desert garden plant. Cold tolerant, it is reported to be hardy to 0°F, and I know that it is grown as far north as Denver. The species forms a stiff rosette with 6- to 8-foot blooming stalks. The flowers range in color from a soft, mossy pink to a hot, vibrant red on a tall spike. They open at various times up and down the stalk, so that the plant is in continuous bloom from late March until September. Yellow forms exist in creamy yellow and bright yellow.

Related species, such as *Hesperaloe funifera, Hesperaloe nocturna,* and *Hesperaloe campanula,* are less common in horticulture but are worth seeking out. *Hesperaloe funifera* has large, spiky, straight leaves over 3 feet long and a blooming stalk well over 12 feet tall. *Hesperaloe nocturna* has fine leaves that give it a grasslike appearance, and its waxy white flowers, as the name suggests, open at night. *Hesperaloe campanulata* is a recently described species that has lovely light coral-pink, bell-shaped flowers. All members of the genus freely hybridize with each other, and some of the hybrids make highly ornamental additions to the garden.

The care of all hesperaloes is reasonably simple. They enjoy full sun and practically any soil, though good drainage helps, as does the odd shot of water in the summer. Red hesperaloe in particular is sometimes slow to grow after transplanting, but extra water will help. Once established, it will form root suckers, thereby creating a clump up to 4 feet wide that produces abundant blooming stalks over the years.

Yucca

Yuccas present more choices than most gardens can accommodate. As a general rule, yuccas fall into two categories: eastern and western. Eastern yuccas—*Yucca gloriosa, Yucca recurvifolia* (also sold as *Yucca pendula*), and *Yucca filamentosa*—have soft, smooth-margined leaves that are often pliable enough to curl. *Yucca aloifolia*, an eastern species common in horticulture, is the exception, with its short, stiff, daggerlike leaves. All these species are slim, either with no rising trunk or a very thin one, and have become common in pot culture and gardens throughout the world. All do well in the desert but require some supplemental water in the summer.

Western yuccas, on the other hand, tend to have hard, stiff leaves, are often huge plants with long leaves, and are more intimidating in a small garden. In addition, there are tropical yuccas—the elegant *Yucca elephantipes* (formerly *Yucca guatemalensis*), which has medium-sized, pliable leaves, and *Yucca valida* and *Yucca filifera*, both with stiff, hard leaves. The latter two require a garden of palatial dimensions, because in maturity they reach heights of 50 feet and spread from their hardened semiwoody base 10 to 12 feet wide.

The western natives are excellent desert garden plants. **Banana yucca** *(Yucca baccata)* and **soaptree yucca** *(Yucca elata)* are fairly common in natural or native gardens. Banana yucca becomes multitrunked in old age and is a moderate-sized blue-gray plant. Soaptree yucca can become large but is irresistibly exciting, with its great blooming stalk rising clear above the foliage.

Perhaps the handsomest yucca of all is the **blue yucca** *(Yucca rigida)*, which has intense blue leaves, creamy white flowers, and a sturdy trunk. Or could it be the vividly green **Mohave yucca** *(Yucca schidigera)* or perhaps the delicate **twisted leaf yucca** *(Yucca rupicola)*, diminutive by yucca standards at barely 2 feet tall and as wide, or its near relative the small blue-gray *Yucca pallida*?

Some yuccas have been in horticulture a long time, and numerous cultivars have resulted. White and cream varieties of *Yucca aloifolia*, *Yucca flaccida*, and *Yucca gloriosa* are commonly found. More colorful cultivars, such as *Yucca filamentosa* 'Bright Edge', are less common but highly desirable.

The western yuccas prefer full sun and extremely well-drained soils, while the eastern yuccas are better in the low desert with a break from the afternoon sun; they also will tolerate much richer, wetter soils. Yuccas customarily maintain a small number of leaves in a rosette on top of the stem, and many hold the old, dead leaves in a skirt around the trunk. This provides some sun protection and is best left alone, as pruning may expose tender tissue to the sun; so be vigilant for sunburn if the dead leaves are pruned routinely.

It is best to plant yuccas young and where you intend for them to grow. Steady watering, once a week in hot weather, helps young plants become established and withstand their first summer. Once the plant is about 2 feet tall, watering can be reduced to twice a month in summer, less in winter. Wells or basins will help watering be thorough and efficient.

Joshua tree *(Yucca brevifolia)* is something of an exception. Although in the low desert even large ones benefit from a monthly deep soak, be careful of too much water in the summer. They are cool-season growers and should be watered mainly at that time.

Transplanting larger yuccas can be tricky. Many, particularly the soaptree *(Yucca elata)*, have a long, deep root, actually an extension of the stem. If this stem is damaged or cut, the plant will die. For this reason, take great care if the plant is large and to be moved; do it carefully and mostly by hand. Allow any small cuts or lesions to heal thoroughly before putting the plant in the ground.

Dasylirion

I can think of nothing more symmetrical than **desert spoon** *(Dasylirion wheeleri)*, a perfect ball of serrated leaves, which has a stem so short and small it hardly exists. The leaves are deep gray-blue, occasionally green, and make a wonderful complement to plantings of succulents or wildflowers; they will also enhance a rugged and rough spot that needs softening. The flowers are not showy but rise on a large stalk like a plume. Old bloom stalks make outstanding walking sticks. The first dried stalks that I ever saw decorated a living room in New Orleans, and I couldn't imagine what exotic and unusual plant must send off such a bloom. The graceful curved stalks remind me of the remnant tusks of a large animal, certainly long extinct and vaguely dangerous.

There are other members of the genus suitable for gardens, including *Dasylirion longissimum*, with its rounded, tubular leaves, and *Dasylirion acrotriche*, which is much greener and finer than desert spoon. While there are still other lovely members of the genus, they can be difficult to locate.

Nolina

I find most nolinas difficult to love, although I am softening. There is nothing wrong with them except they are just a little too much alike and the really interesting ones are large. It makes them challenging in a garden setting, but as the ones in my garden grow in stature, I find my heart growing fonder as well.

Beargrass *(Nolina microcarpa)* is the species most often found in Arizona. It has countless thin leaves and grows 3 feet high and about as wide. This species has a long ethnobotanical history of use in weaving.

A hillside of *Nolina bigelovii* is magnificent. These plants erupt from the dry hills of southern California and western Arizona, rising to 10 feet tall on sturdy, elephantine trunks and bearing branched blooming stalks more than 6 feet long.

Three other species are found occasionally at specialty nurseries or sales. *Nolina nelsoni* has long, fairly stiff leaves and will eventually form a trunk. *Nolina matapensis* has wide, arching leaves and forms its trunk quickly, resembling a small ponytail palm. *Nolina longifolia* is seldom seen but can be an attractive plant in a group, with its long, pliable leaves hanging nearly to the ground from 6- to 8-foot trunks.

The culture of nolinas is uncomplicated. All thrive with summer watering two to three times a month in the low desert but are drought-tolerant if you for-

Nolina matapensis *GARY IRISH*

get. Quite frost hardy throughout the low desert region, they are long-lived and lend an unmistakable flair to a desert garden. Nolinas are good choices around pools, walkways, and dry areas, but keep in mind their large ultimate size.

More Distinctive Plants

Ponytail palm *(Beaucarnea recurvata)* is closely related to the nolinas and is commonly available. It is not a palm at all (another example of an ill-considered common name) and grows into a large plant in a protected spot. Grown best in full morning sun or bright indirect light, ponytail palm can be frost sensitive in the region. The stem flattens and broadens over the years into a great swollen base from which many stems can arise. Thousands of flowers cluster tightly, forming a cream-colored plume. *Beaucarnea stricta,* with its smaller, stiffer leaves, is occasionally found. This species is slightly less cold sensitive.

Manfreda is a small genus in the agave family that is often overlooked for its value in the garden. I find the plants irresistible and have planted one of the pathways in our garden with an ever-increasing selection of them, so that when they bloom, their tall blooming stalks form an honor guard to the lemon tree at the end of the walk. The plants are rosettes of soft, succulent leaves that are fragile and break easily. In some species and their hybrids, the leaves are spotted with dark maroon, which is an odd combination on a plant but is part of their charm.

Manfreda virginica is native to the eastern parts of the United States, but I have little experience with it here. Unlike most other manfredas, it is deciduous in winter. *Manfreda maculosa* is the easiest species to find at the present time. Native to southern Texas, this species has lovely flowers that open wide and are cream colored but fade to a deep old rose. This species is small; the plants are rarely over 4 inches tall and 6 to 8 inches wide, and the inflorescence is 3 feet tall. Most other species of manfreda are much larger, many with blooming stalks up to 8 feet tall.

Manfredas grow extremely well in the shade, even dense shade, in the low desert, need weekly irrigation in summer to look their best, and thrive on sharp drainage. The softness of the rosettes contrasts well with other succulents or with perennials.

I ndex

About the Author

Mary F. Irish is a garden writer, speaker, and consultant in desert horticulture in Scottsdale, Arizona. She is coauthor, with her husband, Gary, of *Agaves, Yuccas and Related Plants*. She has also written numerous articles on desert plants and desert gardening for local, regional, and national publications and has been involved in the electronic media in the Phoenix area, hosting the radio program *Arizona Gardener* and playing an instrumental role in public television specials on desert gardening. She has taught classes and workshops and lectured on desert gardening both locally and throughout the region. Ms. Irish was the Director of Public Horticulture for the Desert Botanical Garden for 11 years, and during that time she managed the Garden's plant sales, plant introduction program, and public horticulture program.